Seeking WISDOM

A Spiritual Manifesto

Wonderful work! Insightful, to the point and in elegant prose, Dr. Culliford's 'manifesto' *describes a program of spiritual development and maturity that can illumine a path for a varied range of human beings who can take action on his prescriptions. I marvel that this psychiatrist-sage's dissemination of his life's studies and experiences is now so encouraging and accessible.*

Jonathan Montaldo, former Director of The Thomas Merton Center, Bellarmine University, Louisville, Kentucky, and author of *A Year with Thomas Merton.*

In cultures riven by opposition politics, Larry Culliford guides us to a common ground, the humanity we share. He follows the wisdom of Thomas Merton who said we must change the world by first understanding and changing our self. This is a concise and lucid study of the stages of development towards maturity, spiritual and human.

Brother Paul Quenon O.C.S.O. poet, writer and monk of the Abbey of Gethsemani, Kentucky, U.S.A.

An urgently important book about a spirituality that transcends the personal search. Suffering is an important step in growing towards maturity, in becoming more and more compassionate and loving. As Larry Culliford points out, not only a spiritual practice is needed but also a re-integration of our "spiritual self", which is more than an ego-bound identity.

Monika Renz, Head of the Psycho-oncology Department at St Gallen Hospital, Switzerland, and author of *Dying: A Transition.*

Larry Culliford offers a clear and useful guide for those seeking personal growth and wisdom in public life. His 'Spiritual Manifesto' is both a gateway into the inner world, and an invitation for further discussion and exploration in the outer world.

Fiona Gardner author of *Precious Thoughts* and *The Only Mind Worth Having*

It is welcome to have a modern reflection of how people today might find wisdom. With his experience as a psychiatrist and his ability to embrace the Christian and other spiritual traditions, Larry Culliford examines how people mature and how healthy maturity leads to wisdom. This skilful author shows himself as a wise teacher whose wisdom needs to be heard.

Dominic Walker OGS, former Bishop of Monmouth

In our time of disorientation and disconnection from our roots, Larry Culliford gives us the benefit of his wise and compassionate insights into the life journey we all share and helpful signposts along the path to genuine responsibility and spiritual maturity. This gem of a book engages readers in an open and accessible way with the essentials of life and the challenges of living, growing, healing and ultimately surrendering all our attachments. Larry invites us to be drawn into a seamless connection to the whole, which is a critical message at every level.

David Lorimer, Programme Director, Scientific and Medical Network.

Books on spirituality tend to focus on deepening the inner life of an individual and their personal search for wisdom. Refreshingly, this book focuses on how a wisdom approach can help individuals manage their outer life and so engage more effectively and purposefully with challenging and complex aspects of human life and society.

The Revd. Canon Rebecca Swyer, Director for Apostolic Life, Diocese of Chichester, UK.

Larry... presents what I would call a matrix; that is, an approach that considers reality from the standpoint of an integration or unifying of all of the various factors in the drama of human life at the present... I see him sketching out in concrete terms the meaning for our actual lives of the matrix itself. How he does it so succinctly and in such a short compass is rather a marvel. Readers of this book will enjoy seeing the whole panorama of this project and I recommend that they engage with it.

Jean McPhail (Sister Gayatriprana), MB ChB, PhD. author of *A Spiral Life*.

Culliford's manifesto reminds us that the promotion of human flourishing should be the goal of a just society. It is an urgent work for an anxious time.

James G. R. Cronin, Vice President for Teaching & Learning, Centre For The Integration of Research, University College Cork, Ireland.

Larry Culliford's call to each one of us to rediscover and nurture our own inner wisdom is just what is needed in these uncertain and challenging times. Whilst seeing clearly the not so pleasant realities of today's world, it offers hope and encouragement that is firmly grounded in research, experience and a balanced perspective. It is through experiencing our spiritual identity and value that we, as individuals, can find the peace of mind and happiness we seek. And only then can the human family as a whole reunite in its vision for a world of truth and harmony. Seeking Wisdom is beautifully written – clear, succinct and with an understanding that is broad as well as deep.

Sister Jayanti, European Director, Brahma Kumaris.

Larry Culliford weaves together a compelling personal narrative about and an insightful psychological evaluation of the times in which we find ourselves, which invites the reader into a deeper appreciation for the intersection of spirituality and science. Culliford provides an array of engaging and interesting insights that will spur reflection and dialogue for all those open to seeking wisdom.

Daniel P. Horan, OFM, Assistant Professor of Systematic Theology and Spirituality, Catholic Theological Union (Chicago, USA)

Seeking WISDOM

A Spiritual Manifesto

Dr. Larry Culliford

The University of Buckingham Press

ISBN 978-1-908684-98-1

CONTENTS

Foreword

Sir Anthony Seldon

In October 1517, Martin Luther challenged the supreme temporal and spiritual authority of his time by criticizing the mercenary priorities of the Pope and the Roman Catholic Church. His widely-disseminated Ninety-five Theses became pivotal in starting the Protestant Reformation. Powerful divisive echoes and after-shocks of that rift permeate world culture today. Now, 500 years later, comes a differently challenging document. This time the force behind it is healing, not divisive. Seeking Wisdom is a unifying text with, at its core, the uplifting message that, 'We are all already one'.

A lifetime writing about prime ministers and others who have reached the top of the tree in politics, business and other fields has led me to one very clear conclusion: neither age, nor power, nor charisma, nor money necessarily lead either to wisdom or happiness.

Since the office was created in 1721, Britain has seen fifty-four prime ministers. Despite having achieved the pinnacle of politics, surprisingly few were happy, nor did they develop happiness after leaving Downing Street. An even smaller number developed any measure of wisdom, perhaps five of the fifty-four, including, in the last one hundred years, and then only at the end of their careers, Winston Churchill and James Callaghan.

It is a consoling thought that power and money often lead away from rather than towards wisdom and happiness. It is consoling, too, to understand that we can all learn to be wise regardless of our standing in life. Humility is a necessary ingredient of wisdom, so it can indeed be easier for those who have least (in worldly terms anyway) to become wise and rich in spirit. The passage from The Bible known as 'The Beatitudes' is just one religious text among many which make this abundantly clear.

In this manifesto, the very experienced writer, psychiatrist and psychologist, Larry Culliford, offers a succinct yet profound road map for how anyone can learn to become a wiser, more mature human being. The approach applies equally to those of any religious faith and none, as long as the seeker is prepared to be open-minded about spiritual progress.

The firmest believers in all religions are seldom, of course, open minded. It would be wonderful if the leaders of all nations on earth, and in all walks of life, were to read this manifesto. We cannot assume that they will. But equally we cannot discount that they might. Whether they do or not is beyond our power. What is within our power is to read and engage fully with this book ourselves, and to have our lives changed significantly for the better by doing so. Our lives will be changed but, more importantly still, so will the lives and opportunities of all those with whom we have dealings and come to influence, in this generation and in generations to come.

Martin Luther disturbed the status quo to its core and precipitated centuries of bloody division and war. With your present mindedness, inspired I would hope by this Spiritual Manifesto, the reverse, a healing and homecoming process, can be initiated. In this way, little by little, the restoration of harmony – at home, in communities, and between people hitherto in conflict – can begin.

Anthony Seldon

DEFINITIONS

Spirit: a word, derived from the Latin *spiritus*, meaning ‘breath’ or ‘wind’, that can be used to denote ‘life force’ or ‘cosmic energy’.

Spirituality: a word sometimes used to refer to human experience ‘wherever the deeply personal meets the universal’. The ‘spiritual dimension’ is better thought of as a kind of adventure playground to explore, affording education and excitement, rather than a specimen to pin down, dissect and analyse.

Holy: a word sharing a common root with *whole* and *heal* (i.e. ‘making whole’) that implies a supreme unifying principle.

The Holy Spirit: is therefore a phrase that can be used to refer to a sacred, all-powerful, unifying life force, or cosmic energy.

Manifesto – a public declaration of attitudes, aims and policies.

DECLARATIONS

To survive constructively, to thrive, a society needs general recourse to language, values and practices associated with spiritual health and maturity.

Within the broadest and most profound limits of human understanding and experience, through a sublimely inspired combination of intellect and intuition, the mysteries and miracles of existence, life, consciousness, love and unity may be fathomed increasingly by all people on the path to spiritual maturity.

INTRODUCTION

Recent elections and referenda have yielded unexpected results. These include the Scottish Independence and Brexit referenda, the Northern Ireland Assembly, US Presidency, and French elections, also two British General Elections. Political parties appear struggling to decide and agree on fixed aims and policies that both appeal to voters and address realistically the challenges of the times. A new degree of flexibility is required that does not fit well with the traditional structures of political life.

Voters are dealing with a greater degree of uncertainty, and a political landscape containing a plethora of powerful vested interests. Leadership that looks strong often turns out to be brittle. Flexible leadership, on the other hand, easily appears malleable and weak.

When leadership is unsatisfactory, a greater responsibility falls upon individual members of society. It becomes necessary to think matters through personally; and this *Spiritual Manifesto* is offered as a discussion document, as a broad-stroke blueprint for people seeking personal growth and wisdom in decision-making. It is not a conventional political statement, because it is not concerned with canvassing for votes in order to take control of the

State. Instead of political *power*, it looks rather towards exerting wide-ranging public *influence*, focusing on informing the general way of life of citizens from all political persuasions.

Such a manifesto, rather than a partisan rallying call, therefore offers suggestions and guidance for unification and harmony. It takes as a starting point that, moment by moment, wisdom seeks what is best for all. In any given situation, it brings people together rather than dividing them. Wisdom necessarily therefore embodies compassion – caring about people; being prepared to suffer with, and on behalf of, others.

'Ultimately, our greatest joy is when we seek to do good for others.'[1]

*

Wisdom can be considered a form of knowledge, but it is different in character from scientific knowledge, the knowledge of facts. Wisdom, rather, is the knowledge of how to be and behave for the best. Like all forms of knowledge and truth, wisdom is sacred. To be sacred means to be inviolable, beyond personal opinions and preferences. It also means to be full of power. Wisdom and spirituality are therefore closely inter-

---

[1] Desmond Tutu in: Dalai Lama, H.H. & Tutu, D. with Abrams, D. (2016).

related. As the remainder of this manifesto will show, the search for wisdom involves an improving degree of spiritual awareness. It is about a person – and, collectively, a community or society – becoming increasingly psychologically and spiritually mature.

To think of oneself as immature can, admittedly, feel uncomfortable. Nevertheless, it is important to recognise – in self and in others – the potential for further growth and development. And it helps to realise that this is a process of nature common to everyone – natural personal, psychological and spiritual evolution – also that, accordingly, it takes time.[2]

It is also necessary to be prepared for the idea that growth of this kind involves engaging with suffering, with all the different types of pain that people encounter: physical, emotional, social and spiritual; from daily minor discomforts to extremes of near-intolerable distress. This *Spiritual Manifesto* speaks not only of how to suffer least, but also of how to make the most of painful experiences – one's own, and those of others. It asserts, too, that the outcome of suffering, when endured and somehow transcended, is wisdom. This means having the increasing capacity for living calmly and joyfully, without destructive

---

[2] For more on spiritual evolution see, for example, Taylor, S. (2017).

levels of painful feelings, without excessive fear, anger or sorrow. However hard won or easily come by, wisdom involves the ability to live contentedly, in a contagious manner that spontaneously informs and influences others, for the benefit of everyone.

This, then, is a public declaration recommending a universal policy of seeking wisdom, both in private and public life, with the patient aim of nothing less than improving life quality for all.

Larry Culliford,
West Sussex,
September 2017

PART ONE

Rationale

We are already one. But we imagine that we are not. And what we have to recover is our original unity. What we have to be is what we are.

Thomas Merton[3]

---

[3] Merton, T. (1973) p 308.

SOME PRELIMINARY IDEAS

For the sake of clarity around the topics of wisdom and spirituality, this section sets out briefly several related sets of ideas forming the basis of the manifesto.[4]

The first set concerns five seamlessly inter-linked dimensions of human understanding and experience:

Physical (energy and matter) – the miracle of existence
Biological (organs and organisms) – the miracle of life
Psychological (mental activity) – the miracle of consciousness
Social (relationships) – the miracle of love
Spiritual (souls and the sacred) – the miracle of unity

Everything concerning human beings – health and sickness, for example – can be seen to operate through all five dimensions. According to this document, the spiritual dimension appears to

---

[4] Readers of this necessarily brief document seeking further clarification will find many of the central issues addressed in earlier books, notably '*Love, Healing and Happiness*', '*The Psychology of Spirituality*' and '*Much Ado about Something*'. See 'References'.

people as embodying an originating principle, seamlessly creating, linking and shaping the other four.

Science seeks factual knowledge through being 'objective', reducing the effects of unreliable human intervention. Reference to *'dimensions of human understanding and experience'*, on the other hand, emphasizes the value of knowledge and experiences that are personal and, in contrast, 'subjective', restoring the individual to the centre of consideration. Dogmatic statements of so-called 'objective' proof are thus avoided. A question like, 'Does God exist?' is unanswerable from this evidence-seeking perspective. Less divisive and more relevant is a question such as, 'Have you, or anyone you know and trust, ever experienced something that seemed like a miracle?' or, 'Have you ever found yourself totally lost in awe and wonder at some aspect of the mysterious workings of nature and the universe?' or, again, 'Have you ever felt yourself in the presence of, or affected by, some kind of divine power or being?'

*

The second set of ideas involves considering life as a journey towards wisdom and maturity, where both good or pleasurable and bad or painful experiences can help people learn and develop through six recognizable stages:

1. *Egocentric* (immature, self-referenced existence)
2. *Conditioning* (learning through insistent and persistent family and social traditions)
3. *Conformist* (seeking to belong by following social conventions)
4. *Individual* (starting to think, speak and act independently)
5. *Integration* (shifting values and behaviour towards altruism, through recognising one's deep kinship with the entirety of humanity)
6. *Universal* (achieving maturity and wisdom, becoming a natural teacher and healer)

There are different tasks, attitudes and priorities at each stage.[5] The first two stages are discussed in the section on 'Education'. The last two appear in more detail in the section 'Towards Maturity'. Because research has shown that the majority of people past their teen years have reached stages three or four, or lie between the two; because in other words, in western society, 'This is where we are', still culturally adolescent; further clarification may be helpful here.

---

[5] See Culliford, L. (2011), also Culliford, L. (2014) The Meaning of Life Diagram: a framework for a developmental path from birth to spiritual maturity. *Journal for the Study of Spirituality,* 4:1, 31-44; also available (free access) at: http://www.maneyonline.com/doi/pdfplus/10.1179/20440243 14Z.00000000019

In explaining the middle stages, it is necessary to emphasise that each person is subject to two contrasting drives:

1. To conform within family and society
2. To think, speak and act independently

In stage three, a person tends to adhere (whether rigidly or flexibly) to the culture, authority, values, belief systems (including religious/secular and political belief systems), laws, customs, allegiances (for example, to a nation or a sports team), rituals and other behavioural practices of the family, communal group and society at large. There is comfort and safety in belonging, with the risk of being ostracised, ridiculed or feeling threatened when showing signs of being different.

Nevertheless, as horizons broaden, contact and familiarity with different people, cultures, conventions, belief systems and so on, may result in review and revision of previous allegiances. Pressure grows to re-think priorities and take increasing responsibility for thoughts, feelings and intentions; also for one's words and actions; equally and importantly, for what one does not say and avoids doing. This is to enter stage four, a key step towards personal maturity; but there is still some distance to travel.

*

A third set of ideas relates to the notion that progress on this journey towards personal maturity occurs most commonly through the transformational effects of suffering. The psychological processes associated with loss, pain, healing and growth will therefore be described in the next section. It follows that, in principle, it is better to face and accept suffering, to make it meaningful and profit from it, rather than seek to avoid it.

This challenges the prevailing attitude within western culture, whereby pain – physical and emotional – is widely considered regrettable, to be eradicated or suppressed. Rather than take responsibility for their own suffering, people are quick to blame other people, corporations or other organisations for not doing enough to prevent or remove pain. It is easier to assume responsibility when the healing process – as natural and reliable, under advantageous conditions, as the healing of cuts, abrasions and fractures – is explained, and a hopeful outcome assured.

Taking personal responsibility – and, therefore, being trained and lovingly encouraged in matters of self-discipline when young, so as to be ready for taking personal responsibility later – is important, because the collective progress of humanity towards wisdom and maturity depends on increasing numbers of people doing so on an individual by individual basis, and generation by generation, until a universal tipping-point may be reached.

Underpinning this is the spiritual concept of 'reciprocity', according to which thoughts, words or actions intending either good or harm – towards another person, group or the environment in which people live – rebound in some way on oneself, for better or worse. It is one of the few principles shared by all the world's major religions, reflected similarly by Buddhist teaching on 'karma' (the so-called 'law of cause and effect') and St Paul's Christian message, 'You reap whatever you sow'.[6] The same idea seems to be expressed in the more colloquial dictum, 'What goes around comes around'.

Wisdom, in other words, suggests that if a person wishes for, intends or does good, acting kindly and thoughtfully, they will benefit. A person who, in contrast, wishes for, intends or actually brings about harm, acting destructively, out of mischief, carelessly or cruelly, will eventually in consequence suffer, but not necessarily in worldly terms. Often unaware of it, they suffer in the spiritual dimension, through diminished contact with the unified cosmic whole, the sacred unity that forms the greatest source of energy, direction, sustenance, courage and hope, through impoverishment, in other words, of the soul.

---

[6] Letter to the Galatians, 6: 7.

People suffer, however, only until they learn and mature. Wisdom recognises the principle of 'reciprocity' not as a punitive mechanism, but as one providing balance and guidance. Apparent misfortune involving loss frequently offers an opportunity for growth. Good fortune at the material level, on the other hand, can easily delay a person's journey towards maturity.

*

A fourth set of ideas forming a thread underpinning this manifesto concerns two complementary ways of thinking, experiencing and interacting with the world. These will be discussed in more detail in the section 'One Brain – Two Ways of Thinking', but it seems appropriate to introduce the distinction between 'binary' and 'unitary' mental activity here.

The binary or 'dualist' approach involves *either/or, black/white, right/wrong, us/them, win/lose, success/failure* type thinking, and is easily, therefore, divisive. The unitary or 'holistic' approach, on the other hand, involves inclusive *both/and* type thinking. It is, therefore, unifying. Materialistic and worldly, dualism is at the heart of human scientific and technical endeavour. The unitary approach, in contrast, informing wisdom and compassion, lies at the heart of human spirituality, seeing people as equals, regardless of gender, sexuality, skin colour, age, race, creed or anything else.

Dualism and holism are both useful and complement each other, but in secular western culture the binary approach has become dominant, resulting in many problems and much human suffering. Personal – and, ultimately, collective – wisdom and maturity depend on a corrective re-balancing where these patterns of thought are concerned. This, too, affects the values adopted by individuals and society, on which there is also a section.

THREAT, LOSS, PAIN, HEALING AND GROWTH

Emotions are vital to a sense of being alive, contributing to an important sense of meaning and purpose. They are valuable indicators of spiritual experience; when people are, for example, 'filled with awe and wonder', 'racked with tears and grief', 'paralysed with fear', 'overwhelmed by a sense of peace and tranquillity', or 'ecstatic with joy'. In terms of this manifesto, emotional sensitivity and self-awareness is at least as important as cognitive intelligence, especially as human emotions operate more logically than is often realised.[7]

Emotions are invested in many things – in people, for example, in places, possessions, activities, in ideas and ideologies. This is 'attachment'. Furthermore, *wanting* to win, for instance, is naturally accompanied by *not wanting* to lose, thus each attachment is accompanied by a corresponding 'aversion'. Attachments and aversions provide the conditions for emotional pain through reversals of fortune. Not having what you desire yields a measure of suffering. Equally, securing one's object of attachment immediately

[7] For a summary of this logic, see Culliford, L. (2014).

sets up the condition of *threat*, the threat of harm, damage or *loss*.

Threats provoke and promote the painful emotions of *bewilderment, anxiety* and *doubt*. Attacks (on one's person, possessions, opinions or beliefs, for example) threaten a form of loss, provoking *anger*. Impending loss engenders feelings of *shame* and *guilt* (through feeling responsible). Actual losses give rise in addition to *sadness*.

Sadness is the essence of healthy grieving. It involves 'letting go', the freeing up and relinquishing of attachments. The cleansing ('catharsis'), of tears and the other accompaniments of grief, permit the loosening ('lysis') of emotional investment in the object of loss, commencing the miracle of healing. As painful feelings die down, each is marvellously transformed into its pain-free complementary opposite. Bewilderment, anxiety and doubt shift towards *clarity, calm* and *certainty*. Anger softens into *acceptance*. Shame and guilt give way to *purity, self-worth* and *innocence*. Sadness is transformed into *joy*. Calm, joyful acceptance of fate is the emotional accompaniment of wisdom.

It is natural for people to resist change, especially in the early stages of spiritual development. Even the threat of change can arouse feelings of anger, which are often accompanied by a strong sense of being right, and of being 'in the right'. This is a destructive (and ultimately self-destructive) trap to avoid. Those who feel right, but are in fact mistaken about something, do well to pause before acting on their emotions. Those who are correct also do well to remain patient in the face of threats and challenges while their anger subsides. They can remain confident that their point of view will be upheld by events as they unfold, and know too that a calmer frame of mind will be more persuasive than a hostile one.

Just as certain conditions must be met for cuts and abrasions to heal, so it is with emotional pain and trauma. Skin is weak and heals poorly in people who are undernourished, lacking essential proteins and vitamins. Wounds do not heal if they are too big or become infected. Doctors and nurses do not heal the damage, but they do ensure the proper conditions; through administering antiseptics and antibiotic medication, for example, and by applying bandaging and sutures.

Emotional healing similarly proceeds best when certain conditions are met. It goes more smoothly when the affected person feels safe from further psychological threats and losses. Protection comes from feeling secure, valued and loved, from living in an environment of affection, trust and hope for the future, and depends therefore on healthy family relationships, and similarly on prevailing, conflict-free community and cultural interactions.

*

Emotional healing carries a valuable bonus. Personal growth towards maturity is a direct and reliable natural consequence. After successfully surviving a loss, people automatically become less fearful of what might happen in the future, less regretful of what has happened in the past, and less anxious generally. They become more spontaneous, better able to live 'in the moment', better equipped to engage anew with people and places, with fresh activities; and better able, too, to sit still and quietly appreciate beauty, to contemplate life's path and ponder its values.

People continue to experience attachments, desires and aversions, and so be susceptible to painful emotions. Nevertheless, experiencing and enduring adversity helps individuals to develop increasing emotional resilience and stability. They grow wiser, calmer, happier, clearer in mind and more confident. They become less inward-looking, angry, guilty and ashamed. Less frequently sorrowful, they nevertheless come to value sadness, when it arises, as a sign of growth; for example, when feeling sad in sympathy with the misfortunes of others.

People who have endured losses also become naturally more outward-looking, thus increasingly aware of the plight and suffering of their fellows, human beings similarly susceptible to attachments, losses, accidents, injuries, mental afflictions, ill-health, ageing – and, finally, death. This new awareness, that everyone suffers, brings life and energy to people's natural tendencies towards empathy and compassion. This insight ensures that people become useful and valuable to others in their suffering.

Knowing that, ultimately, all pain may be shared, makes a person wise, better able to face life's many challenges and vicissitudes, including perhaps the most definitive challenge of dying. Everyone eventually loses all worldly possessions and human connections, being finally called on to relinquish all attachments and aversions as their body ceases to function. Growing in maturity through suffering is good preparation for that. It is a sure sign of maturity when a person can experience emotional suffering – their own and that of other people – without turning away. Another clear indication is the readiness to face death with a smile.

ONE BRAIN – TWO WAYS OF THINKING

The two distinctive 'binary' and 'unitary' types of thinking depend on the human brain having two hemispheres. With upward of 100 billion densely inter-connected nerve cells, according to psychiatrist, neuroscience expert and accomplished author, Iain McGilchrist, 'There may be more connections in the human brain than particles in the known universe'.[8]

The two halves – left and right – are connected to each other by a band of between 300 million and 800 million fibres, the *'corpus callosum'*, yet only about 2 per cent of neurones in the cerebral cortex on each side are linked by these fibres. Furthermore, it turns out that many of the connections in this transverse bundle are inhibitory. They are designed to stop the other hemisphere from interfering. Thus, to a considerable extent, the two half-brains are capable of operating separately, in parallel. They are structurally similar, but have significant differences of emphasis and function; and here is a paradox: although they work

---

[8] McGilchrist, I. (2009) *The Master and his Emissary: The Divided Brain and the Making of the Western World.* New Haven and London: Yale University Press. McGilchrist argues persuasively that, in Western culture, the Master (the right brain) has been deposed by its Emissary (the left brain) resulting in destructive imbalance.

independently, they continuously maintain some contact with each other. Simultaneously, in other words, they work both separately and together. In ideal circumstances, they function as one, a fully harmonised duality working as a united whole.

According to the principle of 'contra-laterality', the left side of the brain controls the right side of the body and vice-versa. Although brain organization varies from individual to individual, regarding left-right distribution of hand-dominance and the contra-lateral location of the speech area, there is considerable consistency.

That the speech centres of the brain are in only one hemisphere forms part of a design in which the left brain tends to deal with 'parts', with pieces of information in isolation, and the right brain with whatever is under consideration as a 'whole'. The left is well-suited to binary thinking, and the right to unitary experience. The silent right brain is attuned to whatever is new, while the speech-capable left depends rather upon what is familiar. In order to appreciate things whole and in their context, the right hemisphere consistently exhibits breadth and flexibility of attention, like a floodlight, compared to the focused intensity of which the left is more capable, like a spotlight.

According to McGilchrist, the human brain must attend to the world in two different ways at once:

> 'In the one (right hemisphere) we *experience* – the live, complex, embodied, world of individual, always unique beings, forever in flux, a net of interdependencies, forming and reforming wholes, a world with which we are deeply connected.
>
> In the other (left hemisphere) we 'experience' our experience in a special way: a 're-presented' version of it, containing now static, separable, bounded, but essentially fragmented entities, grouped into classes, on which predictions can be based. This kind of attention isolates, fixes and makes each thing explicit by bringing it under the spotlight of attention, in doing so it renders things inert, mechanical, lifeless. But it also enables us for the first time to know, and consequently to learn and to make things.'[9]

There are, therefore, two corresponding kinds of 'knowing': knowing *about* things, using the left brain; and a more intimate and personal kind of knowing, using the right. For example, everyone 'knows about' clay, for example, what it is and can be used for; but only a skilled potter or sculptor 'knows' clay well enough, through extensive personal experience, to become one with it and use it, almost as living matter, to create a distinctive

---

[9] McGilchrist (2009) p 31.

object – a simple bowl perhaps – that is both useful and beautiful at the same time.

The two halves of the human brain thus bring two different types of world into being. The left brain has been found to prefer whatever is mechanical, impersonal and abstract. Associated with right hand dominance, as well as the seat of speech and language, it is concerned with making and using tools and machines. The right brain, in contrast, which sees nothing in the abstract, only things in context, takes primary interest in what is living and personal. Appreciating things as whole, it is responsible for recognizing that faces are faces, and as such human, not just juxtapositions of disconnected eyes, nose, mouth *etcetera*, as the left brain would see them. It therefore recognizes people as individuals, a sign of which is its remarkable capacity to appreciate even extremely rapid changes of facial expression.

The evidence firmly suggests that all forms of emotional perception, and most forms of emotional expression, depend on and inform the right hemisphere. This side of the brain is therefore central to satisfactory social interactions, and to those functions and abilities that enable human beings to form bonds – bonds of both attachment (affection, love) and aversion (dislike, hatred) – through emotional understanding and interplay. The right brain, by extension, is also the seat of morality and a sense of justice. As McGilchrist points out, stimuli related to fellow-feeling and co-operation capture the master's right-brain attention, while those related to rivalry and competition are treated in preference by the emissary on the left.

As well as empathy, arrived at through identifying with others, the right hemisphere is also concerned with self-awareness, creativity and intuition. On it depend a number of intrinsically human capacities: the love of poetry, for example, fascination with metaphor, and the enjoyment of imaginative, illustrative stories such as fables and parables. Humour, including irony, satire and sarcasm, also depends on right brain mediated understanding of the context of what is said and done. The right brain alone can recognize and take delight in ambiguity and paradox, double-meanings, and even triple-meanings. Unlike the intolerant left, the right brain lives contentedly with change and uncertainty.

In complete contrast, a dominant left hemisphere, without the moderating influence of the right, results in dehumanisation, in people who will listen but cannot understand; who look but cannot really see. The left brain mediates only the more superficial social forms of emotional expression: the perfunctory smile of acknowledgement, for example, the slight shrug or almost imperceptible raising of the eyebrows.

The left brain is so averse to uncertainty and doubt that it can often cope only by arbitrarily picking just one interpretation as correct. Capable solely of binary (either/or, right/wrong) thinking, it is impatient with all other possibilities, which it construes therefore as wrong. The left brain thus commonly insists it is right, even when mistaken and in the face of evidence. Of the commoner emotions, it notices only anger, so frequently employed to defend the indefensible, a potent but misguided basis for the insistent feeling of 'being in the right'. According to McGilchrist, the left hemisphere supports only, 'A blanket disregard for the feelings, wishes, needs and expectations of others'.[10] This obviously causes serious problems, conflict and suffering as a result.

The left brain is unadventurous. It prefers what is familiar, only discovering more of what it already knows and doing more of what it is already doing. It avoids what is new, unfamiliar and strange. In contrast, the right hemisphere prefers what is new. It is constantly vigilant for change and anomalies. The remedy for an over-bearing left hemisphere therefore involves a powerful corrective balancing influence from the right, because only the right brain can fully grasp the full interplay of the myriad of influences at work in a given situation. The whole brain therefore needs to be in play for full understanding and wisdom to be achieved.

---

[10] McGilchrist (2009), p 58.

The two hemispheres function similarly, but run on markedly different agendas. Over time, these each support and encourage a way of being in the world that is of great value, but which is antithetical to the other. There is, in other words, an apparently perpetual tension or dissonance between the two. The tension can be reduced, however, particularly through a range of spiritual practices, notably meditation, which we will examine in later chapters.

FALSE SELF AND TRUE SELF

A number of authorities have referred to a binary split at the heart of human psychology. One pioneer thinker in this field, Carl Jung, used the terms 'Ego' and 'Self'. Twentieth century spiritual writer, Thomas Merton, wrote about the 'false self' and 'true self'. Others speak of an 'everyday' self and a 'higher' self or 'soul'. Because also used in previous publications, the preferred terms in this manifesto are the *'everyday ego'* and the *'spiritual self'*.[11]

According to the child psychiatrist and researcher, Donald Winnicot, there resides in new-born infants, *'a component of self which possesses a purity, wholeness, untarnished innocence and spontaneity'*, which he referred to as their *'pristine ego'*. Unaffected by attachments and aversions, it is short-lived, however. In the face of urgent and immediate needs – for food, warmth, comfort, safety, affection, etcetera – the early infant ego soon finds itself faced with multiple conflicts and anxieties. Identifying with its body, it soon feels pain, discomfort, frustration, abandonment and emptiness, to the point of insatiability.

This is the early origin of the split between everyday ego and spiritual self. This apparently

[11] See Culliford, L. (2011) & (2015).

binary formula, though, hides the reality that they remain permanently connected as an indivisible unity. Just as a length of elastic, or a guitar string, set in motion, appears to occupy more than one place at a time, due to its rapid fluctuations back and forth, so it is with the apparent dissonance between these two aspects of a person's selfhood. As the arc of life proceeds towards maturity, the apparent split grows wider initially, through the early stages of spiritual development. Later, during 'individual' stage four, it starts to slow, beginning its homecoming reversal during 'integration' stage five, and completing the re-unification process in the final 'universal' stage six.

'Six Stages of Spiritual Development'[12]

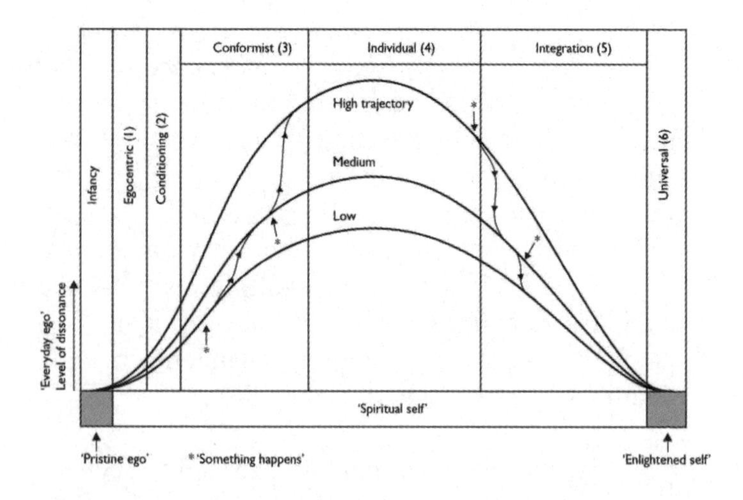

[12] From Culliford, L. (2011) p 160.

People who are inherently more mature, experience less tension and dissidence between 'everyday ego' and 'spiritual self' than do others. The 'high', 'medium' and 'low' trajectories in Diagram 1 indicate that, as life proceeds, some people experience less inner conflict, making developmental progress and transition through the stages more smoothly than others. Innate factors regarding temperament, together with aspects of personal conditioning consequent on the social and familial spiritual environment, determine the general trend for each individual.

Life events and experiences too play a role, whenever 'something happens' of a deeply significant and personal nature to shift a person from a lower towards a higher trajectory or vice-versa. Consider, for example, how a child, raised with a simple Christian belief in the biblical Jesus, capable of healing miracles, may have that faith weakened by an introduction to the principles of science at school. Further imagine that the child's adored parent dies of a painful and debilitating disease, with no healing miracle occurring despite intense prayer. The challenge to that child's belief system will be severe, as innocence becomes tarnished by the experience. Spiritual awareness becomes dulled, more easily ignored as the child's 'everyday ego' shifts to a higher trajectory, towards more material concerns.

Nevertheless, as the diagram's bottom line shows, the spiritual self is never fully extinguished, remaining an influence to account for the important possibility of later re-integration. Imagine now, for example, that the same child experiences, much later, a comforting vision or dream in which the image of the dead parent communicates lovingly that they are well, at peace and free of pain.

This is not unrealistic. Both Thomas Merton[13] and Barack Obama[14] have recorded powerful and meaningful dreams or visions about their dead fathers, occurring when they were young adults. In both cases, the episode was followed by a bout of intense crying, this catharsis being followed by a gradual but permanent change in the direction of their lives and ambitions. Whenever 'something happens' like this to reduce the dissonance between 'true' and 'false' selves, a person's developmental trajectory is spontaneously lowered and readiness to pay attention to one's inner spiritual awareness is rekindled. The consequences show themselves in terms of a healthy change in attitudes and values, of general demeanour, of patterns of speech and behaviour.

*

---

[13] Merton, T (1998), p 123.
[14] Obama, B (2008), p 128 -129.

The 'everyday ego' is the *'me'* people experience most of the time, the personal self that interacts from birth with mother, father, siblings, the wider family and the social group at community, cultural, national and global levels throughout life. People are engaged both with their surroundings, and with the world of inner experience. Through this ego, people form attachments and allegiances. They develop likes and dislikes concerning people, places, objects, activities, sensations, ideas, ideologies, and all manner of things, including much created solely by the imagination.

Driven by the brain's left hemisphere, the everyday ego tends towards being self-centred, unadventurous, materialistic and possessive. Dominated rather by the right hemisphere, the spiritual self, in contrast, is naturally more selfless, creative, intuitive, humble, compassionate and wise. A stranger to desire, it does not form attachments or aversions. Dwelling in the moment, accepting the way things are, it has no sense of lacking anything for itself, while at the same time acknowledging, sharing, and seeking to remedy the many sufferings of others.

There is a sense in which the spiritual self is aware of, and seamlessly connected to, the wider spiritual dimension of being, to the totality, the cosmic whole, to the Sacred Unity that some call 'God' or the 'Holy Spirit', through which each person is connected to everyone else, to everything, throughout the universe and throughout time. The group to which everybody belongs therefore includes the entirety of humanity, living, dead or to come, without exception, and this kinship extends to the creatures of nature, the planet and the universe itself.

Developing maturity involves discovering one's true self, learning to inhabit it to an increasing degree, and so revealing it to others. This means becoming more conscious of what is happening, moment by moment, developing greater discernment, thereby having more choices and the opportunity to be more deliberate in terms of sensible, judicious speech and action, equally (and at least as important) in refraining from unwise, hurtful behaviour. The pinnacle of spiritual development involves a final merging or re-integration of everyday ego and spiritual self in the formation of an 'enlightened' or 'higher' being. There will be more about this again later.

BALANCING CONFLICTING VALUES

Just as it is possible to describe two ways of thinking, mediated by the two hemispheres of the human brain, so is it possible to describe two sets of contrasting, often conflicting, values: 'worldly' and 'spiritual'. The former, summarised by the notion of *power*, are those most frequently adhered to by the false 'everyday ego'; the latter, summarised by the idea and holy ideals of *unconditional love*, are brought to life by the true 'spiritual self'.

Attachment is at the heart of worldly values: the owning of property and possessions, having power and controlling people. Luxury, wealth and fame follow closely. Such values fuel personal and collective aims and ambitions. They are not, in themselves, to be condemned. Worldly success as a result of skill, hard work and determination is often praiseworthy. Nevertheless, when worldly values override spiritual ones, suffering is the result. Success 'at all costs' leads to a culture dominated by secular materialism, mercenary commercialism and ever-expanding consumerism, which necessarily encourage partisanship and rivalry, and therefore inequality and conflict. A worldly attitude involves perpetually seeking opportunities; opportunities for expansion and profit, opportunities to take and remain in control, often at the expense of other people. This is seen as admirable by those in the ascendant during conformist stage three, but comes under question and is ultimately rejected with increasing personal and spiritual maturity.

From a psychological perspective, a primary (often unconscious) underlying motive for preferring worldliness over spirituality involves a strong element of evasion, denial and rejection of suffering – physical, emotional, social and spiritual. Keeping one's left-brain spotlight on 'power', 'success', 'profit' and 'progress' avoids the need to acknowledge, much less take responsibility for, whatever havoc and distress might be visible using the much broader beam of one's right-brain floodlight. This is immaturity.

Mature, spiritual values, on the other hand, embody both wisdom and compassion. Arising with a natural human capacity for love, kinship and fellow-feeling, they represent the truth at the heart of the 'integration' and 'universal' stages five and six, that 'We are all one'; that each person is seamlessly connected through the spiritual dimension to every other person, past, present and future.

Spiritual values therefore include:

- honesty
- trust
- kindness
- generosity

- tolerance
- patience
- perseverance
- joy
- humour
- humility
- gratitude
- dignity
- devotion
- forgiveness
- courage
- compassion
- wisdom
- beauty
- hope.

Only when these values and attributes prevail within a family, community, society or culture, can it be said to be fully healthy. When these values dominate, suffering is much reduced, particularly through being shared and diffused.

The ideal involves a balancing act. A person advertising or selling goods, for example, must balance honesty and generosity with the requirement to promote their wares. It is easier to remain truthful, and to set a fair price, if what you offer is useful, of good quality, robust and genuinely attractive. It is easier to serve others, and profit the community as well as oneself, if you take the trouble to listen patiently, find out what people really need and provide that, rather than products or activities that are unnecessary, may be destructive, risking addiction, for example, or cause harm in other ways.

These values all go together, being inherent in people's true nature. Compassion, for example, is not a choice. It is built-in to one's spiritual self, attuned – consciously or otherwise – to the suffering of others. A choice often made by people during the immature stages of spiritual development is to suppress and ignore it. Wisdom, on the other hand, comes from paying careful attention to painful, as well as pleasurable, stimuli. A number of spiritual practices – both religious and non-religious – can reliably improve one's capacity to do that, to be increasingly mindful in conducting relationships and in going about one's daily business. This topic is also covered further later on.

PART TWO

Commentary

We are what we think… feel… imagine…
All that we are arises in our minds.
With our minds, we make the world.

Speak or act with an impure mind, and trouble will follow you
As the wheel follows the ox that draws the cart.

Speak or act with a pure mind, and happiness will follow you
As your shadow, unshakeable.

The Dhammapada: The Sayings of the Buddha.[15]

---

[15] Adapted from: Byrom, T. translator (1976)

POLITICS

In western cultures, the prevailing model of government involves a parliamentary democracy or similar party system. Safeguards against political tyranny in the UK, for example, include the established existence of a constitutional monarchy, an upper house, a separate judiciary and legal system, and accountable law enforcement agencies. Such a system has been operating for a long time, and still seems adequate, representing an advanced degree of social maturity. Nevertheless, it cannot be deemed completely satisfactory, without room for improvement.

The political scene is changing. In the UK, there are no longer two principal parties (Labour and Conservative) buffered by a third (Liberal/Liberal Democrat), offering opposing options on various issues from which voters can choose. The situation is more complicated, perhaps reflecting a growing diversity of interests and interest groups. It is almost certainly influenced too by the increasing number of people who wish to think important matters through independently; whether from selfish or altruistic motives; and who therefore seek greater flexibility and choice.

One result has been a proliferation of political parties represented in the House of Commons, each with different values, attitudes and agendas.[16] There have always been vested interests, but now there are professional lobbyists and many powerful organisations with vast resources vying for the attention and support of different politicians and political groups. The political views and positions of individuals risk being overwhelmed and discounted by such factions. The maximum five-year life of a government also imposes significant imperatives, as, of course, does the necessity for politicians to gain and retain sufficient votes to hold power at local and national levels.

Although cross-party committees and occasional 'free' votes for Members of Parliament, unrestricted by party allegiances, allow for a degree of harmony, the prevailing mood and manner of British politics – as elsewhere, particularly throughout Europe and North America – is competitive, even combative. Such an environment depends heavily on binary thought processes, involving a mainly left hemisphere driven, oppositional mode of thinking and interaction.

The wisdom view incorporating a more spiritual approach is, in contrast, deliberately unifying. It gives primacy to the individual perspective, being guided by deep personal experience, mediated through (right hemisphere) unitary thinking. It

---

[16] Currently the Green, Scottish National, Democratic Unionist parties, Plaid Cymru and UKIP.

acknowledges the principle of 'reciprocity', and recognises that some degree of suffering is inevitable.

Looking purposefully at all angles, the wisdom view considers what is positive in a given situation alongside what is unsatisfactory before advocating change. It can, when necessary, be decisive, knowing that immediate and sweeping measures are sometimes required in the face of impending catastrophe. It is, however, more often reflective, knowing that changes cause less disruption and suffering when introduced gradually.

The wisdom view, then, is patient. In taking the long-term perspective, it remembers that, where action is under consideration, three options are present, not two:

a) to act
b) to refrain from acting
c) to wait

Waiting allows emotions to settle. Calm, clarity and acceptance emerge increasingly as fear, doubt, confusion and irritation settle. Waiting also allows time for those concerned to investigate the situation further and gain important relevant information in respect of decisions to be made. It allows room for intelligent, unbiased and informed discussion and the wider canvassing of opinion.

The wisdom view takes into account the intense cohesive power of institutions and systems of politics to assimilate even major shifts in circumstances and points of view. It encourages faith that, after a period of instability and uncertainty (such as after a landslide General Election, a significant referendum reversal, or a crash in the economy), the altered political landscape will eventually re-stabilise. Throughout the process, nevertheless, the human condition remains the same. Daily life continues, and people face the same challenges with which to cope, the same threats and losses to face and endure. Everyone must find a way to fulfil their needs and obtain the essentials; especially food, shelter, safety, education and health care, meeting too their needs for occupation, recreation, companionship and a sense of meaning, the feeling that life is worthwhile. The wisdom view considers all these needs paramount.

In this regard, the present political system can take credit for many enduring successes. In 1883, for example, the UK's Slavery Abolition Act was introduced, and in that year too Parliament began voting sums of money annually for the construction of schools for poor children. The Elementary Education Act of 1880 insisted on compulsory school attendance for children from 5 to 10 years old. In 1972, the school leaving age was raised to 16, and the 1988 Education Reform Act introduced the National Curriculum. The UK National Health

Service came into being in 1948, following an Act of Parliament two years earlier. These represent but a few of democracy's crowning achievements.

The wisdom view, based on the principle of reciprocity, in aiming to benefit the greatest number of people, recommends giving the weaker and more disadvantaged members of society pride of place in all political deliberations. Failing to invest sufficiently in compassionate health and social care, for example, including the sympathetic management of criminal offenders, seems unwise, and counts as folly with, otherwise, a high consequent social cost in terms of additional and unnecessary suffering for all.

Folly is the converse of wisdom. It depends on a specific kind of ignorance, the ignorance of context, of the bigger-picture; ignorance derived from the brain's impatient, arrogant, self-serving, narrow-vision, materialistic left hemisphere in contrast to the more settled, altruistic, broad-vision, spiritual right. For example, history has shown repeatedly that the attempt to replace one apparently flawed situation or system of government by another, deemed better – through aggressive incursions, revolutions, map changes (including partition) or any other form of large-scale social engineering – alters but does not necessarily improve matters, often causing considerable widespread disruption and suffering.

Patience, and a gradual, well-informed approach, is usually wiser.

The quality of leadership matters in politics. It makes a difference whether a leader or leading group adhere mainly to worldly or spiritual values, whether in other words they are dominated by *power* on the one hand, or *love* on the other. The issue of leadership is also relevant in the context of large organisations, both secular and religious. The topic will therefore be addressed separately in the following section.

LEADERS AND FOLLOWERS

People in positions of leadership in society arrive by different routes: usually by inheritance, through selection, via promotion, following election, or through self-imposition. Leaders tend to show different qualities according to the different stages of spiritual development. Similarly, people at the different stages seek different qualities in their leaders. Broadly-speaking, the two can be mapped onto each other.

As a general principle, the more spiritually mature a person has become, the less likely they are to seek the power and privilege of a leadership position. A combination of humility and wisdom holds them back. At the other end of the spectrum, dictators impose themselves upon the world, seeking exactly that eminence, commonly exhibiting the attributes of someone stuck throughout adulthood in the primitive 'egocentric' stage one, characterised by a deeply-flawed, narcissistic sense of omnipotence, fierce intolerance of opposition, and a strong predisposition to feelings of persecution.

Those who, as adults, remain at the relatively unquestioning and involuntary 'conditioning' stage two, tend to identify with the strength and apparent self-confidence of such a leader, responding with both fear and excitement to repeated bullying threats and enthralling (but seldom delivered) promises, the sticks and carrots used by such a tyrant to achieve and remain in power.

People at the 'conformist' stage three react similarly, but are more conscious of the risks and benefits of supporting the new leader and regime, uncritically inclined nevertheless to catch the wave and kowtow. People at the 'independent' stage four can go either way. They may be more likely to rebel and offer resistance to corrupt leadership, but some will seek to join the regime, without ceding their true loyalty (which remains self-centred), seeing it as an opportunity for personal gain.

People in the more mature stages also face options: to rise up in opposition and risk martyrdom, or bide their time and avoid confrontation, helping the regime's victims where possible, remaining confident of a better future, thereby instilling courage and offering hope.

*

A commoner picture in western democratic culture is of essentially conformist leadership. In a two-party system, the strength of each party will attract followers from people in the early stages of spiritual development, not yet ready to take a full measure of personal responsibility for what happens. While party allegiances may remain relatively fixed, leading players come and go, largely depending on the level of political success or failure with which they are associated.

With increasing numbers of people reaching independent stage four, however, there is a greater call for accountability among the leadership, also for broader choice and greater creativity. Caution is required, though, because of dangers associated with widespread 'individualism', with a kind of 'I know better' attitude among a populace often critical of any leadership expecting discipline and obedience. The risks are of localised ungovernability and even larger-scale anarchy. Such independent-minded people require highly skilled leaders, able to recognise these tendencies. In dealing with them, it is necessary for those in authority to be transparent and flexible, providing timely information of good quality, and to display sound reasoning about the matter under consideration. It is best to consider all possibilities and offer creative alternatives, to foster independent thinking and discussion on the topic, and listen to everyone involved (including both the powerful and marginalised), while being prepared all-along either to act decisively in everyone's best interest, to refrain from action, or to encourage patience and wait.

The preference of more mature people, those who have entered 'integration' stage five and 'universal' stage six, would be for leaders at least as spiritually advanced and mature as themselves. Whereas they often have a natural aptitude for recognising wisdom and compassion – or the want of them – in those seeking political office, it is also true that spiritually mature people tend to be relatively unconcerned about external leadership within society. Their focus is more on the internal leadership and guidance found in paying close attention to the inherent wisdom of their sacred inner compass, the 'spiritual self'. When they experience dissatisfaction, they are inclined to regard it more as signalling an opportunity for personal growth than as a need for leadership action and external change.

Similar issues to those discussed in this section regarding leadership and politics are played out, with distinctive variations, in the separate but linked arenas, for example, of religion, education, health and social care, and economics, to be covered in the following sections.

RELIGION

The relationship between human spirituality and organised religion is complex. One approach considers the former as a unifying dimension of personal and collective experience, and the latter as centred on the social dimension, influencing people in different ways, capable of polarising them completely. To use a metaphor, spirituality can be thought of as the vital and nourishing central root of a great tree, the main branches of which represent different world religions. The smaller branches in turn represent smaller scale denominations of the major religions and faith traditions.

Even atheistic belief systems can have roots in the spiritual dimension, as attested by the many people who consider themselves *'spiritual but not religious'*. This attitude often involves emphasizing negative aspects of religion, for example that it has served as an ultra-conservative and repressive influence, has led to social and cultural divisions, and been the excuse for barbaric warfare, torture and executions. At the personal level, it has resulted in psychological hardship and damage, a source of exaggerated guilt, fear and anxiety. Dogmatic teaching on ways of thinking and behaving have hindered educational development, led to rigid and punitive parental styles, justified unfair and pernicious social stratification, led to unnatural and repressive attitudes towards the body and sexual relations, and hindered creative expression.

Against this, supporters of religion point out that it has also inspired many noble acts of self-sacrifice and altruism, stimulated great art and architecture, motivated people to develop moral and ethical systems, and, through its institutions, been a guardian and force behind learning, health care, commerce and other major activities, with a remarkable legacy of universities, schools, hospitals and social welfare.[17]

According to the scheme of this manifesto, the two sides of religion, destructive and creative, can be explained in terms of contrasting immature and mature spiritual development, from which people averse to organised religion are not necessarily exempt. One researcher in America has described five types of 'spiritual-but-not-religious' attitudes:

Dissenters – critical of religion,
Casuals – who consider spiritual practices as of value because leading mainly towards better health, stress relief and emotional support,
Explorers – seeking novelty and new experiences without settling,

[17] See: Fontana, D. (2003)

Seekers – decidedly looking for a fresh spiritual home,
Immigrants – in the pre-commitment process of adjusting to a new spiritual home or community.[18]

Elements of conformist stage three and individual stage four mindsets can be identified among such people, who will also include individuals oscillating between the two or temporarily stuck in tension between these contrasting stages.

When a person has started moving away from the family and home community tradition, this plays out in some cases in attempting to return and convince others to follow the new path they have discovered. Understandable though this may be, it often serves only to promote conflict and delay such a person's progress towards the more enlightened stages five and six.[19] This predicament may similarly transpire whenever ardent adherents to any cause (religious, political or otherwise) seek prematurely to 'convert' others. In extreme cases, there may be compulsion with threats and punishments – even torture and death – for those who resist. The mature approach – confident that a wise, compassionate attitude is wholly more convincing than an aggressive one – is more patient and tolerant, seeking to promote genuine personal

[18] See Mercadante, L.A. (2014).
[19] See Culliford, L. (2011) pp 105-11 & 153-161.

transformation and progress on the spiritual journey, rather than superficial mass change.

Regarding spiritual development, Christian writer, Richard Rohr, emphasizes the *'journey into the second half of our own lives'* that awaits everybody. He says that, although everybody gets older, not everyone sets out on this second half of the pilgrimage, or makes it very far. He calls this further journey a well-kept secret, of which too few are aware. *'People at any age'*, he says, *'Must know about the whole arc of their life and where it is tending and leading'.*[20] With this knowledge, decisions become easier to make and carry out in both halves of life.

According to Rohr, the first half involves 'surviving successfully', by establishing an identity, home-base, family and friends, livelihood, regular pastimes and so on: the essential aspects of community and security. For the majority of people, this is all there is, valuing a sense of belonging, and prizing what is familiar and habitual. But Rohr criticizes: *'Most of us are never told that we can set out from the known and familiar to take on a further journey. Our institutions and expectations, including our churches, are almost entirely configured to*

---

[20] Rohr (2012), pp vii - viii.

encourage, support, reward, and validate the tasks of the first half of life.'[21]

In expressing his disappointment, Rohr makes clear in contrast that some people, even young people, do become aware of and accept the challenge to move forward, to escape the gravitational pull of conformity, to take responsibility and work towards spiritual maturity. Religious organisations seldom promote this, however. A conformist attitude prevails, to the extent that people who think for themselves and ask questions, trying for example to square scientific discoveries with time-honoured spiritual teachings and truths, are given inadequate encouragement or support. It can be seen then as natural, even admirable, when such a person turns away from organised religion and religious teachers who fail them in this way.

This may well change as religious leaders grow to understand the process better, attending fervently to their own spiritual development, becoming more tolerant and flexible, encouraging independent-mindedness, letting people move away without considering it regrettable or a failure, and being better prepared to welcome such individuals back into active roles within the faith community when they are clearly working towards spiritual maturity.

---

[21] Rohr (2012), p xvii.

Most world religions have already mapped out well-trodden spiritual pathways, the paths of mystics, saints and gurus. Holy men and women past and present from Judaism, Christianity, Islam (Sufism), Buddhism, Hinduism, Sikhism, Taoism, Jainism and other traditions have demonstrated this. Such wise and compassionate people have much in common, particularly the use of silence, stillness and solitude, and the practice of meditation or silent prayer.[22]

There is much to be learned too about spiritual maturity from elders and skilled practitioners of the ways and lore of surviving indigenous populations.[23] There is a paradox at work in many tribal cultures. Adolescent boys and girls are required to mature into adult members of their close-knit community, to become increasingly capable of independence of thought, word and action, and of taking responsibility, without either leaving or damaging the integrity of the tribe. A system of 'initiation' enables this development, characterised by the learning of traditions, specific knowledge and skills, and by the facing of challenges. For the boys, these tend to be based mainly on hunting; for the girls, on childbirth. When completed successfully, the initiate is rewarded in a special ceremony, a 'rite of passage'.

---

[22] See Culliford, L. (2015) pp 191-8.
[23] See, for example, Nerburn, K. (2017)

Until teaching and leadership on more advanced aspects of the spiritual path are better provided by a person's culture or religion of origin, individuals in western society have no alternative but to seek wisdom elsewhere, taking responsibility for themselves. As the 'everyday ego' comes increasingly under the influence of the 'spiritual self', the inner imperative to do this grows accordingly. Life becomes akin to a pilgrimage, with an inherent sense of mission and the revival of a sense of honouring one's truest self.

It seems surprising that relatively few people living in a secular western culture reach such a turning point, and make such a commitment to seeking wisdom, when one considers the positive relationship of children to the spiritual dimension, as explored in the following section.

EDUCATION

Research into childhood spirituality was wrong-footed in the 1960s by an intellectual bias, until researchers began listening to what the children said without imposing their own interpretations on their narratives. According to more recent research, though often invisible to the adult world, it is normal for children to have rich and varied spiritual lives, which serve to underpin altruistic and ethical behaviour, guiding children towards enduring meaning, purpose and connectedness throughout life. Aspects of children's spirituality may also help when losses and other forms of adversity are encountered.

Children's spirituality involves moments of reverence, awe, delight and wonder, may concern the afterlife and life's ultimate questions, tends to include religious experiences, and may also involve a darker side of spiritual experience. Hay & Nye[24] were able to identify a common thread, a core category to which they gave the name, 'relational consciousness', similar to the idea of 'spiritual awareness'. The two main aspects of this category are:

1. During private interviews with a specially trained researcher, the children demonstrated an

---

[24] Hay, D. & Nye, R. (2006)

unusual level of consciousness or perceptiveness, compared with during other passages of conversation.

2. The conversation was expressed in terms of four particular types of special quality relationship with:

    a) Things,
    b) Other people,
    c) The child himself or herself,
    d) God.

Older children were found to reflect more intentionally on their thoughts, feelings and experiences, such that it was often an *objective* insight into their *subjective* responses that gave them a new dimension of understanding, meaning and experience.

These researchers found that many children are able to develop a positive identity and sense of purpose through awareness of being part of something far greater than themselves. Some of the children seemed to have given up their use of religious language and spiritual imagery because it apparently failed to capture the inherent complexity and mystery the children wanted to convey. The attempt was therefore discarded. Instead, their spiritual awareness still intact, they turned to other means of expression.

The critical observation made by numerous researchers concerns, however, that a reduction in spiritual awareness and expression has been found, in industrialized societies, to be normal among older children (above 10 to 12 years approximately). As they encounter both religious scepticism and the traditions of science, these young people are under intense pressure to conform to the prevailing secular worldview.

At 'conditioning' stage two, children naturally respond to the powerful influences and imperatives of families, teachers and peer groups. It follows then that children's spiritual awareness needs to be discovered, acknowledged and nurtured by adults – especially parents, grandparents and teachers – if they are to grow into whole-minded people who are not only cognitively, but also socially, emotionally and spiritually developed. The 'Catch-22' is that adults who are not yet sufficiently spiritually mature themselves may struggle to recognise and encourage the spirituality of the children in their care.

As a result of this conditioned dampening, awareness of and preoccupation with the spiritual dimension fade and disappear from children's lives. Receiving limited encouragement and having no adequate language of expression, many children's capacity for spiritual awareness atrophies to the point of vanishing. The residue goes to ground and lies dormant unless and until 'something happens' to rekindle it.

These observations have considerable significance, not only for the education of children, but also for the progress of adults towards spiritual maturity, a process likely to have stalled due to early and involuntary, secular conditioning.

Education (from the Latin *e-ducere*, meaning 'to lead out') involves helping children discover and bring forth knowledge and wisdom from within, rather than simply the imposition and learning of facts and skills. Time for both reverie and play is, therefore, essential for the spiritual well-being of children, who need to reflect, play out and work through the many problematic issues that confront them, day by day. The most satisfactory curriculum therefore fosters a balance between learning facts and making sense of experiences; between left and right brain functioning, in other words. Meditation, which harmonises left-right brain activity, is therefore useful for this.

There is good evidence that children introduced in school to regular meditation (also called 'stilling') even for short periods once or twice daily, benefit through improvement in conduct, enhanced learning ability, creativity and imagination, and have better relations with their peers and teachers.[25]

---

[25] See, for example, Campion, J. & Rocco, S. (2009), also

They are calmer, happier and more mature, learning about the value of co-operation as well as that of competition; learning to respect their rivals, becoming increasingly appreciative of the opportunities that different opponents present them for self-development. It is a very mature position to encounter and experience a supposed 'enemy', not as someone to either avoid or annihilate, but as a valuable teacher.[26]

Many schoolteachers make an effort to retain, express and share regularly their own sense of wonder concerning the subjects they teach, rather than reduce it to text book summaries and the dull repetition of 'facts' for later regurgitation by pupils in their exams. This is necessary and appropriate when aiming to foster, rather than inhibit, the inherent spiritual tendency of children to greet nature and respond to it with awe, amazement, delight and a genuine sense of mystery. From the perspective of this manifesto, it is especially for science teachers to ensure that science and spirituality remain in harmony for each child.

---

www.meditationinschools.org and
www.mindfulnessinschools.org.

[26] See Rabten, G. & Dhargyey, G.N. (1977), for example (p 17) 'When someone whom I have assisted/And in whom I have placed great hope/Inflicts me with extremely bad harm/I shall view him as my supreme spiritual friend'.

HEALTH, MENTAL HEALTH AND SOCIAL CARE

Compared with the Victorian era, health and social services in western democracies are relatively advanced. Screening and other sickness prevention programmes, for example, demonstrate a high degree of social maturity. At the worldly level, they reveal financial acumen, warding off the risk of greater subsequent costs by discovering and treating problems at an early stage. At the spiritual level, they embody a marked degree of kindness and compassion, allowing people to feel more secure in regard to their health as they advance through life.

Matters are less clear-cut, though, when for example a person's liberty is removed (albeit temporarily) under Mental Health legislation if, through mental illness, they are at risk of self-harm or behaving in a dangerous manner. It is clearly in the best interests of the community for such a person to be 'sectioned' and removed, but it is only in that person's best interest if they then receive high quality assessment, treatment and care in a safe, nurturing environment, attended to by skilled staff, and released again, not prematurely, but only when mental health has been restored.

It is costly to provide this level of mental health care, and it requires much more than financial expenditure. It requires suitable buildings, which may be affordable, but it also needs large numbers of mental health professionals: doctors, nurses, social workers, psychologists, occupational therapists, pharmacists, administrators and others. This is not only about financial expense, therefore; it is also about self-sacrifice. All of these people commit themselves to years of training. On low incomes, they usually incur a degree of personal debt, but only one aspect of their sacrifice concerns money. They will face high levels of hard to remedy, human suffering on a more or less daily basis.

From the worldly perspective, the training received, together with regular subsequent financial remuneration and the promise of a healthy pension, provide considerable incentives; but these benefits are easily undermined within a hierarchical organisation governed by financial and political targets, where the good of the organisation apparently (despite often worthy 'mission statements') takes precedence over the welfare of the individual, whether staff member, patient or a patient's family members. The situation worsens further when recruitment problems add to the burden of workload, which threatens quickly to become excessive; and worsens again whenever pay fails to keep pace with inflation, making the job less attractive, and making recruitment even harder.

Because, whether anxious, depressed, demented, deluded, hallucinating or ‘acting out’ in a destructive or self-destructive manner, people experiencing mental illness are challenging to look after, another dimension of self-sacrifice is called for, deep personal commitment to the well-being of patients. This is a challenge because, without wisdom and compassion, it is easy to fall prey to fatigue, frustration, cruelty and despair. It is difficult, in other words, to maintain the required levels of energy, courage, kindness and hope. Compassion – ‘suffering with’ others in their distress – needs tempering with the wisdom that recognises the need for adequate time for recovery and revival, for rest and re-creation. The care-giver’s first priority is, paradoxically, to care properly for oneself. A vital aspect of this, particularly for the more spiritually mature and insightful, is likely to involve engaging in regular forms of spiritual practice, to ensure continuing progress along the pathway to wisdom. There will be more about this in Part 3.

Much the same applies to those working with people (especially with children) who have physical health problems, facing disfigurement, for example, permanent or recurrent pain or disability, or with people in great distress and anguish, possibly as a result of treatment or through being terminally ill. Somehow, though, for many people, however difficult and emotionally painful this work becomes, when faced with a mature and enduring combination of acceptance, calm, faith and hope, it can seem extremely worthwhile.

It sometimes happens that, at an early age, a person 'knows' that they are destined to become, for example, a doctor or a nurse. This is 'vocation', a spiritual experience involving a sense of being called to do something selfless, great and useful to others. Implicit in accepting such a calling is the faith that one has the predisposing character, intelligence and aptitude for the training and the challenges to follow, and that somehow, whenever needed, through a kind of 'grace', motivation, energy, guidance and strength will be found, coming from within. The inner determination to succeed in gaining the required qualifications, and to master the required skills, depends on one's essentially spiritual conviction that all is meant to be (through 'karma', perhaps, or 'God's will'), and that nothing can or will stand in one's way. When barriers arise, they too are seen as part of the process, to be overcome with persistence or circumvented with wisdom.

Such a journey is, in a sense, its own reward. Regular remuneration, and later a pension, are pleasing but not central considerations. Even success with patients is a secondary feature, on account of knowing that nature heals and health professionals only assist in the natural process; also because one counter-balancing failure can offset many successes.

Day by day, year by year, the most satisfying reward for commitment to helping others is a sense of growth, of becoming increasingly true to one's higher nature, to one's 'spiritual self', giving in less readily to the worldly temptations of a hedonistic life and the lures of luxury, wealth, power and fame. From the first day at medical or nursing school, the health care student is faced with the facts of human suffering – physical, psychological, social and spiritual. In western culture, the emphasis is on scientific knowledge, on related diagnostic and other technology, and on pharmaceuticals and surgery to assess, correct and cure symptoms, to suppress physical and emotional pain. Progress along these lines has been phenomenal, and is to be applauded. Curing symptoms, however, is not the same as healing people. To heal, in this context, means 'to make whole', and this is essentially spiritual work, requiring a different, complementary approach.

Students are largely discouraged from thinking and enquiring about patients whose condition – medical, surgical or psychiatric – cannot be cured or much improved. They are asked to trust and accept blindly that science will one day find the necessary solution. Worldly values prevail, and specialties that promise speedy and effective treatments – surgery, in particular – are considered more praiseworthy, are more popular, and are better remunerated than those dealing with more intractable problems, for example dermatology, rheumatology, neurology and psychiatry. The wisdom approach, however, would be to re-balance this situation, aware that equally valuable but different skills and personal characteristics are required in the different situations.

Even from a worldly viewpoint, helping to keep a young person with schizophrenia functioning in society, with his or her symptoms under reasonable control for most of a lifetime, is arguably of at least as much value to the community as the surgical repair of an injury that enables an adult to return to the work-force. From the spiritual perspective, though, there is the additional benefit *to the practitioner* of engaging fully with the same patients over a period (a situation which used to be common in general practice when whole families, generation by generation, were signed up with and treated by a single GP). The opportunities for personal growth are more abundant here than during the brief, often relatively impersonal, encounters between today's health care professionals and their patients.

Such matters are seldom put for discussion before medical or nursing students, who may develop their own preferences and inclinations, but this could be a missed opportunity. Third-year medical students who have attended for teaching about spirituality and health care, for example, reported the following:

- Although the 'holistic' or 'bio-psycho-social' approach to healthcare dominated the rhetoric of the teaching they had received, spirituality was not usually mentioned.

- Previously equating spirituality exclusively with religion, after the course students recognised a clear distinction between the two,

- Also that a person's spirituality is not dependent on religious affiliation, conviction or practice.

- Hesitant to discuss spirituality with their teachers and colleagues before the course, students much preferred afterwards being open, feeling adequately equipped now to discuss the subject.

- Before, neither religion nor spirituality were considered by students to have a place in modern, scientific, evidence-based medicine. Afterwards, they considered patients' spirituality important, recommending that it be assessed routinely. They said that all healthcare staff should be able to 'take a spiritual history'[27], as they had learned to do, so that appropriate steps could be initiated to meet patients' spiritual needs where possible.

- Students reported that taking a spiritual history alone seemed to benefit some patients. One reported, for example, 'I have been a medical student for three years and that's the first time I have come away feeling I've actually helped somebody.' [28]

By the end of the short course, students were also able to demonstrate a satisfactory general overview of spiritual and religious factors that might affect health or the course of an illness. The idea that people continue to grow spiritually through life, especially through adversity, resonated positively with several students. Some reported regretting previously neglecting their own spiritual development. Some, who had been having doubts about its relevance to their careers in medicine, expressed their gratitude and relief, saying the course had rekindled optimism, giving the spiritual dimension renewed importance in following their chosen career.

Such observations show how widely, almost universally, the secular, materialistic, left-brain

---

[27] See, Culliford, L. (2007a).
[28] See Culliford, L. (2009).

approach has been adopted in the field of health care, but also how quickly such perceptive students can firstly recognise the incompleteness of the teaching, then make up the deficit. The spiritual approach is not contrary to the more typical, binary, sick/well medical model of health care. It is complementary, enhancing it, and is of special value whenever the limits of traditional medicine and surgery have been reached, when anyone is facing disfigurement, disability, dementia, for example, or death.

According to Monika Renz, a psychotherapist and spiritual caregiver, who works with dying patients as head of the psycho-oncology department of a large hospital in St Gallen, Switzerland:

> 'Dying persons undergo a transition, which consists essentially of a transformation of perception. As we approach death, all egoism and ego-centred perception (what I wanted, thought felt), and all ego-based needs fade into the background. Coming to the fore is another world, state of consciousness, sensitivity, and thus another way of experiencing being, relationship, connectedness, and dignity. All this occurs irrespective of the individual's worldview and faith.'[29]

[29] Renz, M. (2015) p 17. See also Renz, M. (2016).

This final phase of life continues to be of value as people continue growing until their final breath. Renz's observations echo the research of psychologists Reza Arasteh[30] and Steve Taylor[31], for example, who found similar changes indicating marked shifts forward in terms of spiritual development in people facing or following extreme ego-threatening situations.

Hospices, as well as hospitals, can therefore be considered valuable places to work, volunteer or simply visit, acting as informal 'spiritual universities', treasure-houses of spiritual experience. That they are the focus of, and owe their continuing existence to, an immense amount of charity work, adds to their value within communities. Some hospices have recognised the broader context of their work and provide outreach facilities, including some hosting a 'schools project'. This offers a short, structured series of visits for groups of about a dozen ten-to-twelve-year-old children with their teachers, who meet and engage with patients, family members and staff, volunteers and perhaps also recently bereaved people in a safe, supportive and fully supervised environment that is said, perhaps surprisingly, to promise 'lots of fun and laughter'. Such projects, in addressing myths and reducing anxiety around loss and bereavement, help create in children, and in

---

[30] See: Arasteh, A.R. (1975)
[31] See: Taylor, S. (2011)

parents (who are invited to attend one of the sessions), healthier attitudes towards death, dying and life transition. Like other related outreach projects, they also build links and raise awareness in the community about the hospice's work and purpose.

As might be expected from observations about children's innate spiritual awareness, the schools project conveners describe a heart-warming honesty, directness and openness among their young visitors. *'They handle it better than many grown-ups'*, was a typical comment. Respecting the inherent wisdom and spiritual integrity of children is a key element of this manifesto.

CAPITALISM – ECONOMICS, BANKING AND BUSINESS

The apparent clash between worldly and spiritual values that features in the context of health and social care is even more marked in regard to economics, banking and business.

Capitalism, an integral and largely beneficial aspect of western democracy, involves private wealth being used to provide services, or to produce and sell goods, for financial profit. The system is enabled by the stock market, and by banks offering loans and mortgages, also in the interests of making profit. The necessary promotion of consumerism accounts for the universal use of advertising and other forms of commercial inducement, which lead directly to a widespread general preoccupation with such goods and services. While the 'spiritual self' remains relatively unmoved, such a system is mightily appealing to the 'everyday ego'. Capitalism thus implicitly promotes immature, worldly values to those who are susceptible. As such, it risks a proliferation of desire, greed, excess and wastage on one hand, scarcity, debt, poverty and inequality on the other.

People up to the 'conformist' stage three, in seeking to belong, do not want to miss out or feel left behind by their peer group. They usually want to keep up, for example by having many 'followers' and being much 'liked' on social media. They also have a strong tendency to *worry*: about what other people think of them, about their appearance, their social status, their wealth (or lack of it), and much more. It is a fallacy, fed by commerce and advertising, that freedom from worry and lasting contentment come when a person has whatever they want in terms of wealth, position and an associated abundance of everyday goods and services. The need to defend one's position and protect one's possessions is energy-sapping. Envy and resentment are rife. Excess often results in satiety and boredom, triggering a near-perpetual search for novelty and stimulation. The success of commercial advertising depends upon this. Adverts are specifically designed, 'To create an anxiety relieved by a purchase'; this notion underpinning the unkindest of fallacies on which the capitalist system is based.

Internet companies have also learned to target individuals with personalized advertising based on computer analysis of their 'likes' and other preferences. Goods and services are presented ever more seductively as so-called 'click-bait'; and a particularly unwise form of advertising preys on whatever residual spiritual awareness exists within a person, corrupting the fragile flame of maturity through the use of spiritual and religious ideas and images (icons), to promote luxury goods; chocolates, perfumes, holidays and fast cars, for example, none of which are either necessary or spiritually beneficial.

In order to keep up with the temptations spread before them, people become convinced they 'need' things, rather than simply 'desire' them. To be able to buy the desired goods and services, a preoccupation with personal income and job security becomes an overriding concern. The level of disquiet is heightened for those who are poor, also for those with debts and mortgages. This anxiety, in turn, sets the scene for rivalry between people seeking limited work opportunities, resulting in strong antipathy towards strangers and immigrants, for example, characterised unfairly as undeserving interlopers.

Rifts arise too between employees and their employers, whose jobs and (usually higher) incomes depend in turn on maintaining commercial profitability. Work, rather than being a creative and fulfilling aspect of an individual's daily life, part of one's spiritual journey, risks becoming only a means to an end, the simple goal of livelihood at the personal and family level, the means to pay for both necessary and superfluous (but desirable) goods and services. The goals at the level of the employing organisation and the wider political state include principally commercial success and 'wealth creation' to provide perpetual economic growth.

On the positive side, there are countless ways in which capitalism has brought benefits to individuals and society, not least through free or subsidised housing, education and health care, also military and police protection, fire and sea rescue services, public transport and many other civic amenities, such as effective sewerage and waste disposal. It is also very encouraging to be aware of the extraordinary beneficence of wealthy philanthropists, and the immense amount of beneficial work of many types conducted by many well-supported charities. These too can be seen as integral to the capitalist way of life. It will undoubtedly be unpopular, therefore, to indicate and dwell on the flaws inherent in such a money-and-goods obsessed system. In the interests of wisdom and maturity, though, it must be admitted that there are destructive consequences of consumerism. A significant number of inter-related ills can be seen to affect society as a direct or indirect effect of the imperatives inherent in such an apparently relentlessly profit-motivated attitude whenever spiritual values are subordinated to worldly ones.

To begin with, precious minerals, plants and forests, fossil fuels and other natural resources are required in abundance to feed western economies, and large amounts of inert or noxious waste products must be disposed of or recycled. The tendency is for resource-poor countries and territories to be neglected, and resource-rich lands to be plundered by those states and organisations already rich and powerful. Negative consequences include the possibility of political upheaval and armed conflict, also the grave threat of ecological damage.

Goods and services provided by political states, often in combination with private enterprise, include the weapons and delivery systems of war, so-called 'defence', and other forms of aggression, together with multiple back-up services. These reap enormous and relied-upon contributions to the economy, risking a heedless hunt for financial gain that may easily over-ride important other considerations, and compromise severely spiritual values and the universal search for wisdom.

Armed aggression often results in large numbers of destitute and dependent refugees. Other consequences of capitalist economics and the huge international corporations of 'big business' may also include global warming, climate change and unstable weather patterns, leading to an increase in natural catastrophes (like hurricanes, floods, famine, forest fires and coastal destruction due to melting polar ice and rising sea levels), with a further resulting increase in the numbers of disaster victims and refugees.

Closer to home, well-intentioned but relatively spiritually immature people in the absence of meaningful and satisfying employment, may suffer a kind of 'spiritual malaise', falling prey to symptoms like anxiety and depression, reducing further their likelihood of finding and holding onto a job. Comfort-eating may lead to obesity. Smoking causes heart disease and cancer; and a range of other destructive addictions lie in wait for those who seek distraction from tedium, people concerned not with spiritual comfort and personal development, but with the ultimately futile attempt to numb or avoid physical and emotional pain and suffering.

Addictions are extreme forms of attachment, and frequently indicate a degree of spiritual immaturity and distress. While some addictions are less harmful than others (running, for example, or playing bridge), others are exceptionally destructive, hurting not only those affected, but also their friends and family, and the wider community. The most harmful include addictions to sex, gambling, nicotine, alcohol, and other drugs like heroin and cocaine. These, in turn, give rise to another level of social destruction through crime, particularly 'organised crime', which preys especially on vulnerable people. Such crime includes people trafficking, modern slavery, forced prostitution; drug production, smuggling and selling; money laundering, and tax evasion. Often, these go together.

Policing these matters is difficult and expensive. Offenders, when caught, require and deserve punishment, but also understanding and skilled rehabilitation. This, too, to reduce re-offending, is in society's best interest. Investment in addicts and offenders when young, still at school age, seems likely to yield the most beneficial results, so it is discouraging to read of significant school drop-out rates, a rise in gang conflict, acid attacks, gun and knife crime among teenagers, and an official description of child offender units as 'unsafe'. One hopeful prediction, however, is that – with advancing spiritual maturity among the population at large, generation by generation – such tragic problems and the associated suffering are likely gradually to fade away.

*

Light and dark balance each other. The wisdom approach is to see all the social ills and benefits of capitalism as seamlessly inter-related. For the present and immediate future, it is necessary to accept that one aspect goes with the other, like night and day. For improvement to occur, from the spiritual perspective, it is a question once again of restoring a balance between worldly and spiritual values. That a spiritual, rather than worldly, deficiency is involved in addiction behaviour, for example, is supported by the relative success of the 12-step method pioneered by 'Alcoholics Anonymous' and similar organisations for drug addicts, gamblers and other groups.[32] This involves affected people making, *'A decision to turn our will and lives over to the care of God* as we understand Him', *'Asking Him humbly to remove our shortcomings'*, and, *'Seeking through prayer and meditation to improve our conscious contact with God, praying only for knowledge of His will for us and the power to carry that out'* (from steps 3, 7 & 11). The phrase, *'As we understand Him'*, is interpreted very broadly within these organisations, not necessarily from a Christian perspective. The invoking of some form of spiritual assistance and intervention is, however, definitely intended.

To repeat, rather than government-led social engineering, the best way forward involves individuals committing themselves to making progress, and helping others make similar progress, towards wisdom and maturity. Many people, consciously or unconsciously, carry out some form of Spiritual Development Plan or Programme (SDP), starting out on the journey of the second half of their lives, exploring profitably the spiritual dimension of human understanding and experience. Part 3 looks more closely into that highly recommendable option.

---

[32] See Alcoholics Anonymous (2001).

ART

Art forms a living bridge between the psychological and spiritual dimensions of human experience, between mind and spirit. This is the primary reason why artists create, and the rest of us value their art.

It is important to make a clear distinction between art and merchandise. Wisdom avoids materialist contamination of true art; of artistic creations that reflect spiritual principles and values like beauty, creativity, honesty, generosity, discernment, patience and perseverance. To situate art in the market-place can easily result in spiritually impoverished ephemera, the production of which is governed by worldly priorities like profit, success, power, status and fame.

The 20th century monk and spiritual writer, Thomas Merton (whose parents were both artists, and who was himself a notable poet, calligrapher and photographer), wrote in a letter to Boris Pasternak in October 1958, *'I do not insist on this division between spirituality and art, for I think that even things that are not patently spiritual if they come from the heart of a spiritual person are spiritual'*.

If art comes from the heart and, likewise, speaks to the heart, this asks something of the witness too. It requires a kind of emotional and spiritual sensitivity with which to receive the generous gift of the artist.

I remember, for example, some years ago, standing transfixed before a self-portrait of an older Rembrandt in an exhibition in London. It was hot and crowded in that dark, airless space. I was aware of people coming and going beside me, but remained standing there in a kind of timeless personal bubble, filled with fascination and wonder. I also recall a similar experience when, as a teenager on a family holiday in Spain, I heard on the radio for the first time Rodrigo's magnificent 'Concerto de Aranjuez'. Entranced, delighted and awestruck for the entire duration of the piece, I did not want it to end. These were not simply aesthetic experiences – moments of pleasure. They were, I would say, spiritual experiences, because they were in some small way transformative. I was not entirely the same person afterwards but somehow indefinably wiser and better connected, through the art and the artist, to the entirety of humanity and the cosmic whole. I consider it proof of this assertion that the most vivid and delightful memory of these and other similar experiences has stayed with me ever since.

In Part Three, there is some discussion about 'Spiritual Practices' that people might engage in regularly, to further their journey on the path of spiritual growth and development. These include, *'appreciation of the arts and engaging in creative activities'.* Another is, *'reading poetry and literature'*, in which case the left hemisphere of the brain is required to read the words, and the right to provide context and imagery. People who read music or lyrics, which they then play or sing, are similarly powerfully harmonizing the left and right brains. A third form of spiritual practice listed is therefore, *'engaging with music'*, and this includes listening, chanting and dancing, as well as playing and singing.

This might involve sacred music, but not necessarily. Many forms and styles of music are capable of releasing something profoundly emotional – some sadness, perhaps, or great joy – that has been imprisoned hitherto by excessive attention to worldly concerns and the busy pursuit of secular activities. Rhythmical and repetitive dance (like that of the Sufi dervishes) and chanting (whether Gregorian or the kirtan[33] and bhajans, for example, of the sacred Hindu and Jain traditions), bringing left and right brain together – in a way similar to the effect of meditation – form a powerful bridge between a particular form of art and deeply personal spiritual experience. Furthermore, people coming together to engage in such practices, as when playing in an orchestra or singing in a choir, may well experience

[33] For information about kirtan chanting see, for example, Nikki Slade's website: www.freetheinnervoice.com.

enhancement – through sharing – of the potential for spiritual gain.

This is further testimony to the principle that everyone is connected to everyone else through the spiritual dimension of experience. *'We are already one'*, as Thomas Merton once wrote, *'But we imagine that we are not. And what we have to recover is our original unity... What we have to be is what we are'*.[34] Art can help us do that.

---

[34] Merton, T. (1973) p 308.

PART THREE

Seeking Wisdom

Do not be conformed to this world, but be transformed by the renewing of your minds, so that you may discern the will of God – what is good and acceptable and perfect.

St. Paul: Letter to the Romans 12: 2.

TOWARDS MATURITY

Faced with an extensive daily diet of human suffering, fed out twenty-four hours daily through the media, a person's first impulse is often 'to do something'. The next is to call on others to do something, people in positions of authority and power. A great deal is done, and done charitably, when both natural and man-made disasters occur, but onlookers necessarily remain aware of much untouched and irresolvable anguish and misery in the aftermath. Not everything can be prevented in the first place or put right afterwards.

This leaves many such bystanders at risk of despair, a negative frame of mind that involves powerful feelings of dissatisfaction, anger, guilt and shame. If asked, 'Where is the pain?' many will point to the catastrophe on the television screen and say, *'Out there... Look!'* It is better, though, for people to remain reflective, recognising that the only pain they can take responsibility for and deal with directly lies within their own hearts and minds. The way forward is to permit feelings of grief to surface; in other words, to identify with the suffering of others and lament.

This is one of the first and most valuable lessons when seeking wisdom and maturity. In the face of suffering, it is necessary to become aware of the painful emotions that arise in the face of loss; to feel okay, if possible, without adding an extra layer by feeling bad about them. It is necessary, in other words, to cultivate an attitude of acceptance, to allow the full interplay of feelings into consciousness, including sadness and the accompanying release of tears, so that nature's solution, the natural processes of healing and growth, can begin working towards fruition. This also means restraining oneself from speaking out or acting in response to any destructive or self-destructive impulses provoked through painful emotions, notably fear, anger or guilt.

When the pain is closer to home – a person's own suffering, or that of a beloved family member, for example – a shift in perspective, from anguish and misery to wisdom and compassion, depends on recognising and feeling genuinely, with a true heart, that others elsewhere are suffering too. Such a change brings the comforting knowledge that one is not alone, prompting the healing idea that all human suffering may be shared.

According to this manifesto, then, it is not enough for people simply to conform within society. It is not even enough to seek independence, taking some measure of individual responsibility for one's intentions, words and actions. It is necessary to go further along life's journey, experiencing oneself as seamlessly connected to the whole, to everyone else, to nature and the fullness of creation.

Making progress on the spiritual path into the second half of life, going past stages three and four, beyond self-centred egocentricity towards selfless universality, comes about largely through letting go, releasing both attachments and aversions. This is more difficult and painful in the earlier stages, when people hold on tightly to what they have and what they believe. With growing maturity, it becomes clearer that relinquishing a degree of attachment does not necessarily involve losing the object of attachment entirely. This subtle distinction makes things easier, allowing people to continue the enjoyment of specific objects, places, activities, ideas, and even relations with other people, without being as rigid and possessive about them as before. Maturity delivers rewards because, in giving up attachments and, particularly, aversions, the process becomes increasingly liberating. Letting go is accompanied more frequently by feelings of relief, joy and laughter in place of grieving, sorrow and tears.

With maturity, particularly from 'integration' stage five onwards, a kind of 'homecoming' begins. The tension between one's false 'everyday ego' and true 'spiritual self' diminishes. It is usually a gradual process, but sometimes occurs following a breakthrough spiritual experience, an epiphany, during which 'something happens', something inexplicable, beyond words. Such a breakthrough is hard to predict and plan for, but progress – gradual or sudden – is more likely when someone adopts a formal or informal 'Spiritual Development Programme', consisting of one or more regularly engaged in spiritual practices.

*

Spiritual practices can be divided into two main types: religious and secular. They are of time-honoured value, and have in common that they improve harmony, restoring an ideal balance between the left and right brain hemispheres, and so between spiritual and worldly values. Spiritual practices promote personal equanimity in the face of threats, also grieving and healing from losses, with personal growth as a natural and irreversible consequence. Between people, even people from widely different backgrounds, who may not even have a common language, shared spiritual practices tend to promote fellow-feeling.

The simplest SDP might consist of a daily routine of three parts:

a) Regular quiet time (for meditation, reflection or prayer),
b) Appropriate study (of religious or spiritual material),
c) Maintaining supportive friendships with others who share similar spiritual aims and values.

The value of stillness and silence, often coupled with solitude, cannot be over-emphasized. *'Simply being with yourself'*, is the essence of the practice of meditation, silent prayer, mindfulness, or 'stilling', which involves focused concentration on a stable, unobtrusive stimulus – such as one's own breath flowing back and forth, or a simple sound, phrase or prayer.

Importantly, one's mind is allowed to settle, so that internal as well as external stimulation softens and the mind begins to focus upon itself – to notice without disturbance the thoughts, emotions, sense perceptions and impulses that arise. Eventually, even residual mental content subsides, leaving the mind entirely clear and alert.

This 'mindful' mental state, devoid of the 'everyday ego', is expansive and full of energy. It can seem endless or bottomless, yet there is no partitioning within it, and no room for anything else. This is the essence of unitary, 'holistic' experience, the natural state of the 'spiritual self', fully in tune with the universe.

The benefits are cumulative, as practitioners persist and skill is acquired; and they extend well outside the meditation sessions. Even short periods of regular mindfulness practice can reshape the brain's neural pathways, increasing those areas associated with kindness, compassion and rationality, while decreasing those involved with anxiety, worry and impulsiveness.

Meditation involves more than simply employing various techniques. It is a mysterious process that occurs spontaneously as a gap opens up when the mind becomes engaged purely with itself, a time during which it is more likely that 'something happens' than during everyday waking consciousness. The only way to assess the benefits, and to achieve its precious fruit, is to engage and persevere with the practice oneself, to undertake it rigorously, like any scientific experiment. To try out meditation therefore involves acting in faith. Not quite identical to religious faith, this is faith in some aspect of nature that can confidently be predicted, like the healing of a flesh wound, or the changing sequence of the seasons.

Meditation forms a key component of the mystical paths of most world religions, but it is increasingly used too by those who count themselves atheist or 'spiritual but not religious'. It seems safe to assume that people who are religious and people who are not religious experience similar promptings from their inner compass or guide, impulses for spiritual self-improvement arising from uncomfortable tension between the 'everyday ego' and the 'spiritual self'. To cater for this, a number of other religious spiritual practices also have secular counterparts.

Religious practices, in addition to meditation and prayer, include:

a) Worship and other forms of ritual practices
b) Reading scripture and theology
c) Listening to, singing and playing sacred music
d) Undertaking spiritual retreats
e) Going on pilgrimages to sacred sites
f) Through service, doing vocational and charitable work

Their secular equivalents include:

g) Folk traditions and rituals
h) Contemplative reading of poetry, philosophy, fine literature and good quality self-help advice
i) Engaging with uplifting or 'soulful' music – through listening, singing, chanting, playing and dancing
j) Through regular acts of kindness and compassion

Whether religious or not, people utilise additional similar methods of spiritual refreshment and renewal, often combined. These include:

k) Maintaining stable and loving family relationships and friendships
l) Engaging with and enjoying nature – connecting in various ways with the sea and the countryside, in parklands and gardens
m) Physical activity and keeping healthy
n) Appreciation of the arts and engaging in creative activities

Just as people come together in churches, synagogues, mosques, temples and gurdwaras, not only to cement their faith and worship but also to engage in community activities and communal life, so do secular groupings arise to engage in co-operative activities of a sporting, recreational, charitable or other type in ways that involve a special quality of non-partisan bonding and friendship. When spiritual values are adopted and adhered to, harm is avoided and great benefit possible.

With increasing spiritual maturity, both religious devotion and civic duty feel less like burdensome servitude, more like joyful liberation. If these rewards are not felt, though, as is often the case with the newly committed, a temptation may grow to abandon the intention to adopt regular spiritual practices. Seeking the company and support of others on the spiritual path helps offset this. Reading encouraging stories about spiritual masters, teachers, heroes and heroines, who have persevered in the face of great challenges, offers another way forward when discouragement threatens… But not everyone is ready for this; an idea provoking thought about how one individual can best try to help another who seems to be struggling or actively resisting. It is best to avoid turning away from the ignorance and suffering of others, but it may be necessary to protect oneself if they are behaving in a threateningly destructive manner. Even then, one may be able to learn from and make use of their opposition, as long as it is not totally overwhelming. It is worth bearing constantly in mind, however, the most important requirement: to give priority to one's own spiritual progress. Everything else will then follow.

*

APPEAL

Because one's own spiritual progress must take priority, the main appeal and recommendation of this manifesto is addressed to people individually, rather than collectively, and it has two-stages:

a) Firstly, for each citizen to take personal stock, taking time to think about life in the long-term, about one's priorities and values, and so assess one's position on the pathway to spiritual maturity,

b) Secondly, for each then to become a committed wisdom-seeker or *'soul-smith'*, by attempting to identify and follow their unique individual pathway to wisdom, perhaps seeking a vocation, and certainly by adopting a Spiritual Development Programme of some kind, giving up attachments and aversions along the way, growing naturally closer to others day by day, week by week, year by year.

This would be to set a magnificent example, encouraging others to do likewise as the fruits of one's spiritual practice shine forth, radiating outwards into the community. It is best to seek help early on, advice and encouragement from those already wise and mature, but spiritual guides are not widespread or easily identifiable in western culture. False guides (often excessively self-promoting) also present a significant problem. It may be necessary to discover reliable methods, implement a plan, and forge ahead for oneself.

In making any self-assessment, it is important to be honest, equally to avoid false modesty. The most telling and helpful question to keep asking is, simply, '*Who am I?*' The obvious answer is, '*I am a person, a human being*', followed by details as follows:

One's names, place of birth, where you live, nationality, race, primary language (including accent or dialect), sexual orientation and preferences, social class, religious (or non-religious) affiliation, and/or political persuasion.

People also identify themselves as family members (parent, sibling, child, aunt, uncle and so on), and according to marital status. Other relevant details include levels of education, income and wealth, health/illness status, type of work, preferred style of dress, diet, hobbies, preferences for music and media viewing, sports interests and other matters.

All of this more or less pins a person down, the kind of information that helps others to know *about* them, but not necessarily to *know* 'who they really are', to encounter their essence and feel a loving bond of devotion. Other questions are needed, like, '*What else motivates you at the deepest level?*' and, '*Where do you draw strength, courage and hope from, when you face challenges... when times are really hard*?' These are more spiritual questions.

There are different life priorities for people at different stages of spiritual development, as follows:

Egocentric stage 1: is concerned principally with safety, survival and comfort, seeking to fulfil personal likes and dislikes.

Conditioning stage 2: involves learning, absorbing knowledge – about the world in general, and especially about traditions, rules and conventions. It is a period of dependency.

Conformist stage 3: reflects consolidation of one's attachments and aversions in the interests of personal gratification and social integration, through acquiring prized allegiances, status and possessions, also through denial and rejection of whatever seems alien and contradictory. The 'everyday ego' remains dominant, in discordant tension with the 'spiritual self'.

Independent stage 4: involves discovering and developing oneself as an independent and responsible observer-participant in one's own life, loosening or relinquishing former attachments and adjusting to the resulting uncertainty and relative isolation.

Integration stage 5: involves re-evaluation of one's values and behaviour from a universal perspective, bringing one's life increasingly into line with the highest of altruistic ideals. The 'spiritual self' grows increasingly influential as the force of the 'everyday ego' weakens.

Universal stage 6: involves realising (making real) life's *intrinsic* meaning. One's seamless connection to the whole is firmly grasped and fully accepted. Many attachments and aversions are relinquished. Being, rather than doing or achieving, takes priority. This stage involves living in the moment, not preoccupied with regrets for the past or anticipation of the future. There is no fear of further loss, or even of death.[35]

*

Given the dominance of worldly, materialist values in capitalist democracies, and given the dearth of spiritual teachers, there is a further appeal to spiritually-minded individuals, especially those vocationally associated with state powers, religious organisations, large corporations, the media and other powerful agencies influencing public opinions, attitudes and behaviour. The task before you involves working towards change; by instituting and encouraging discussion about the benefits of a spiritual worldview, and by

[35] Adapted from Culliford, L. (2014).

championing a renewed primacy of spiritual over worldly values.

It seems appropriate, for example, to re-emphasize the value of rest and recreation. A day filled with eight hours each of work, rest and play, together with a shared day off at the weekend to cultivate inner peace, and thereby outer harmony and fellowship, will also allow people to prioritise and develop SDP's side by side.

While always respecting boys' and girls' innate wisdom and personal character strengths, it is also appropriate – given children's high degree of receptivity during the conditioning stage – to infuse them with patterns of politeness, respect for other people, good manners, kindness and other spiritual values.

It is worth noting the particular importance of restraint. It is not being mean or lacking generosity, for example, to withhold inessentials from a child (or anyone else). This is being wise, even noble, as is firm encouragement in regard to saying 'please' and 'thank-you', for example, and maintaining personal dignity. All these matters can be taught by instruction, but are better taught in addition by consistent example. Although they may not immediately seem connected to spirituality, they can on reflection be seen to exemplify the essential truth at the heart of this manifesto – the unity of humanity: 'We are all one'.

This is a principle worth instilling in young and old alike, in anyone not yet sufficiently mature and insightful on the matter. It is the same principle of reciprocity that forms the basis of the Golden Rule, to *'Do as you would be done by'*, and the scriptural advice to *'Love your enemies'*. This is not to be construed as weakness, as the immature are tempted to do, but as sound psychology and wisdom. To bear a grudge, to think badly of any person for any reason, to harbour less than fully kind and generous feelings and intentions towards anybody, is more *self*-destructive than harmful to others.

To be a victim of severe physical torture and mental torment, to the brutal extent of rape or murder, is extremely unfortunate; but deliberately to perform lesser injuries on another can be counted worse by far, amounting to committing in addition an unparalleled form of psychological and spiritual self-harm, by cutting oneself off from the sacred whole, from whatever makes life truly meaningful. Until some form of redemption may be found, one risks lingering in a state of soul death, a victim of utter loss and despair.

To ward against the emergence of a powerful, selfish 'everyday ego', and reduce to a minimum the risk of subsequent spiritual deficiency, it is worth restating that it seems particularly important to foster the inherent spiritual awareness and sensibilities of children, for example through encouraging schools and teachers to undertake meditation or 'stilling' sessions regularly with classes, and to help convey a sense of mystery and a spirit of awe, wonder and delight in subjects, while also giving out facts and teaching skills. Teachers and parents are also likely to benefit from this approach. As time passes and the children involved grow through adolescence to adulthood and maturity, everyone else in society is likely to benefit too, in a process that will then be repeated more easily generation by generation.

The way a native tribe benefits when indigenous youths mature into adults through initiation programmes is not replicated in western society. The Scouts and Guides movements, and the UK's Duke of Edinburgh Awards scheme, offer something comparable, as less formally do apprenticeships, university placements, Voluntary Service Overseas, the US Peace Corps, and military service. These all provide opportunities to develop self-discipline (while fostering various degrees of either conformity or independence), and lead to experiences of important, possibly challenging, differences through encountering other people and seeing how they live their lives. A 'gap year' period of work or travel offers a similar opportunity. There is plenty of scope to develop more satisfactory and better recognised 'rites of passage' for young people, giving them the chance to develop maturity and wisdom, earning them rewards of status and respect within society. At the same time, for the good of the whole, those many young citizens currently denied or unsuited to such opportunities must not be neglected. Viable alternatives are also required to include as many as possible, especially the disadvantaged – those at high risk of poverty, educational deficiency, unemployment, delinquency, addictions, crime and imprisonment.

At the other end of the age scale, people who are old, ill, demented and dying require equally caring attention. The spiritual perspective insists that each person has a part to play throughout life. It resolutely considers all the challenges presented by the elderly as opportunities. Faith in human compassion, courage and creativity may confidently be called upon to address and resolve difficult and distressing situations, large and small, as people continue to grow *through* pain and change, rather than by seeking to avoid them.

*

Backed by sound reasoning, this manifesto and these appeals offer hope, for as long as people respond favourably. The document ends here with a reminder that' its aim is to prompt extensive, fruitful discussion. A second aim is to provide a sound initial basis for the many who resolve personally to investigate the universal mysteries and miracles of existence, life, consciousness, love and unity, and so embark upon a new start in life, seeking wisdom.

***

ABOUT THE AUTHOR

Larry Culliford trained in medicine at St Catharine's College, Cambridge and Guy's Hospital, London, worked in hospital medicine and general practice in UK, New Zealand and Australia, and later qualified as a psychiatrist, working until retirement in the UK National Health Service. Fascinated by the vital question, 'What is mental health?' he began thinking and writing on the subject in the late 1970s, eventually publishing books and articles on happiness, psychology and spirituality.[36]

Larry was raised from childhood in the Anglican Christian tradition. His religious development involved first leaving and later returning to Christian practice.[37] An independent and original thinker, since becoming increasingly aware of the spiritual dimension of human experience, he has sometimes referred to himself as a 'universalist Christian', being open, thoughtfully, to the teachings and practices of both other world faith traditions and spiritually-minded secularists.[38] For

---

[36] See: www.ldc52.co.uk.

[37] See Culliford, L. (2016) *Much Ado about Something* – Afterword: 'My Christian Journey'. London, SPCK.

[38] See Culliford, L. (2007) *Love, Healing & Happiness* – Appendix One: 'Universalist Religions'. Winchester, O Books.

example, in the early 1980s, he spent time studying with Tibetan Buddhist monks from whom he learned much of value, including how to meditate.

To paraphrase the Christian spiritual writer, Thomas Merton,[39] by whose life and work he has been strongly influenced, Larry says:

> 'I will be a better Christian, not if I can refute all the other religions, but if I can affirm the truth in them and still go further. There may be much that one cannot fully 'affirm' and 'accept,' but first one must say 'yes' where one really can… If I affirm myself as a Christian merely by denying all that is Muslim, Jewish, Protestant, Hindu, Buddhist, etc., in the end I will find that there is not much left for me to affirm, and certainly no breath of the Holy Spirit with which to affirm it.'[40]

Conscious that spirituality transcends all religious boundaries, working with patients and colleagues from all the world faiths and none, Larry became aware that a widely-acceptable non-denominational language of spirituality was required, in order fully to explore this vital aspect of physical, mental and social health. Spirituality is an essential element of

---

[39] See: www.merton.org.

[40] Adapted from Merton, T. (1966) *Conjectures of a Guilty Bystander.* New York, Doubleday & Co., p129.

human and social psychology, a crucial – if largely invisible and significantly under-estimated – factor in everyday life. This short book summarises many of the lessons he has learned during his lifelong attempt to seek wisdom.

Larry was a co-founder of the Royal College of Psychiatrists' *Spirituality and Psychiatry* special interest group. He is a former Chair of the 'Thomas Merton Society of Great Britain and Ireland'. He is a long-term member of both the 'Scientific and Medical Network' and the 'British Association for the Study of Spirituality' (BASS). He is also a life-member of the 'Movement for the Abolition of War'. He is currently a volunteer with the Schools Project at St Barnabas Hospice in Worthing.

REFERENCES, RECOMMENDED READING AND WEBSITES

Books and Papers:

Alcoholics Anonymous (2001) New York: Alcoholics Anonymous World Services Inc., 4th edition.

Arasteh, A.R. (1975) *Toward Final Personality Integration: A Measure for Health, Social Change, and Leadership*, 2nd edition. New York and London: Wiley.

Byrom, T. translator (1976) *The Dhammapada: The Sayings of the Buddha.* London: Rider Books.

Culliford, L. (2007a) 'Taking a Spiritual History', *Advances in Psychiatric Treatment*, 13:3, 212-19.

Culliford, L. (2007b) *Love, Healing and Happiness: Spiritual Wisdom for Secular Times*. Winchester and Washington: O Books.

Culliford, L. (2009) 'Teaching Spirituality and Health Care to Third Year Medical Students', *The Clinical Teacher*, 6:1, 22-7.

Culliford, L. (2011) *The Psychology of Spirituality: an Introduction.* London and Philadelphia: Jessica Kingsley Publishers.

Culliford, L. (2014) The Meaning of Life Diagram: A Framework for a Developmental Path from Birth to Spiritual Maturity. *Journal for the Study of Spirituality,* 4:1, 31-44.

Culliford, L. (2015) *Much Ado about Something: a Vision of Christian Maturity*. London: SPCK.

Dalai Lama, H.H. & Tutu, D. with Abrams, D. (2016) *The Book of Joy: Lasting Happiness in a Changing World.* London: Hutchinson.
Fontana, D. (2003) *Psychology, Religion and Spirituality,* Oxford: BPS Blackwell.
McGilchrist, I. (2009) *The Master and his Emissary: the Divided Brain and the Making of the Western World.* New Haven and London: Yale University Press.
Mercadante, L.A. (2014) B*elief without Borders: Inside the Minds of the Spiritual but not Religious.* New York: Oxford University Press.
Merton, T. (1998) *The Seven Storey Mountain,* fiftieth anniversary edition. New York: Harcourt, Brace & Company.
Merton, T. (1973) *The Asian Journal*, ed. Naomi Burton Stone, Brother Patrick Hart and James Laughlin. New York: New Directions.
Nerburn, K. (2017) *Neither Wolf nor Dog.* Edinburgh: Canongate.
Obama, B. (2008) *Dreams from my Father.* London: Canongate.
Rabten, G. & Dhargyey, G.N. (1977) *Advice from a Spiritual Friend.* New Delhi: Publications for Wisdom Culture.
Renz, M. (2016) *Dying: A Transition*, translated by Kyburz, M. & Peck, J. New York: Columbia University Press.
Renz, M. (2017) *Hope and Grace: Spiritual Experiences in Severe Distress, Illness and Dying.* London and Philadelphia: Jessica Kingsley Publishers.

Rohr, R. (2012) F*alling Upward: A Spirituality for the Two Halves of Life.* London: SPCK.

Taylor, S. (2011) *Out of the Darkness: From Turmoil to Transformation.* London: Hay House.

Taylor, S. (2017) *The Leap: the Psychology of Spiritual Awakening.* Navato. CA, New World Library.

Websites:

Author's blog:
www.psychologytoday.com/blog/spiritual-wisdom-secular-times

Author's website: www.ldc52.co.uk

BASS (British Association for the Study of Spirituality): www.basspirituality.org.uk

International Thomas Merton Society:
www.merton.org

Kirtan Chanting (Nikki Slade):
www.freetheinnervoice.com

Meditation in Schools:
www.meditationinschools.org.

Mental health leaflet:
www.rcpsych.ac.uk/healthadvice/treatmentswellbeing/spirituality.aspx

Mindfulness in Schools:
www.mindfulnessinschools.org.

Royal College of Psychiatrists' Spirituality and Psychiatry *Special Interest Group*:
www.rcpsych.ac.uk/spirit

Scientific and Medical Network:
www.scimednet.org

Thomas Merton Society of Great Britain and Ireland: www.thomasmertonsociety.org.uk